OLD-FASHIONED
FLOWERS

Classic Blossoms to
Grow in Your Garden

Tovah Martin-Guest Editor

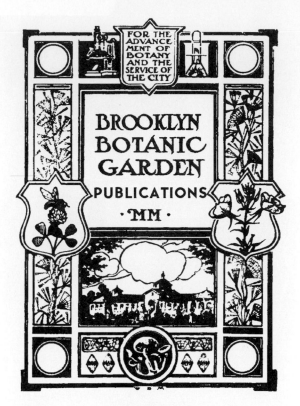

Janet Marinelli
SERIES EDITOR

Beth Hanson
CONSULTING EDITOR

Anne Garland
ART DIRECTOR

Mark Tebbitt
SCIENCE EDITOR

Judith D. Zuk
PRESIDENT

Elizabeth Scholtz
DIRECTOR EMERITUS

Handbook #162
Copyright © Spring 2000 by the Brooklyn Botanic Garden, Inc.
Handbooks in the *21st-Century Gardening Series,* formerly *Plants & Gardens,*
are published quarterly at 1000 Washington Ave., Brooklyn, NY 11225.
Subscription included in Brooklyn Botanic Garden subscriber membership dues ($35.00 per year).
ISSN # 0362-5850   ISBN # 1-889538-15-9
Printed by Science Press, a division of the Mack Printing Group.
Printed on recycled paper.

TABLE OF CONTENTS

INTRODUCTION

SAVING OUR FLORAL HERITAGE

TOVAH MARTIN

FOR SOME REASON, I've always been interested in plants from the past. If a flower was pretty, I admired its beauty. If a plant had handsome foliage, I valued that virtue. But if there was a story behind a plant—if it had roots deep in history—then I was truly intrigued. Even if it lacked the bright colors, the compact growth habit, and the easily controlled demeanor of its modern counterparts, I liked the plant because it was old.

There's an enchantment to old-fashioned flowers. They were the blossoms that furnished our ancestors with food, medicines, cleaning aids, and insect repellants. They were the blooms that the pioneers brought with them across the country. And they provided the inspiration for poetry, the emblems for political movements, and the bouquets for lovers. They fostered myths and legends; they were the fodder for old wives' tales and superstitions.

According to Scott Kunst of Old House Gardens, heirlooms are some of the hardiest plants in the garden. Certainly, many vintage flowers have survived over the centuries, stubbornly staying in cultivation despite the ebbs and flows of fashion. And fashion has often been the enemy of heirlooms.

Thanks to the efforts of a handful of preservationists, old-fashioned flowers are still available. In this handbook, a few of the activists in this growing field share their knowledge. They are the foot soldiers of the movement, working to ensure that vintage flowers do not disappear—and that the stories surrounding heirlooms do not slip away. While enrolled in the Longwood Garden Program through the University of Delaware, Peggy Cornett of the Thomas Jefferson Center for Historic Plants spent years thumbing through dog-eared period catalogs, studying the fluctuations in popularity of annuals between 1865 and 1914. Christie White of Old Sturbridge Village has devoted equally long hours to seeking out references

4

for vintage vines. Ellen McLelland Lesser went to art museums and libraries, looking for hints in oil paintings to teach her how flowers were used in arrangements before the 20th century. Every contributor to this handbook has made an equally important contribution to our wealth of knowledge of the past.

The author's cottage garden. By growing vintage varieties, we can help preserve our floral heritage.

Choosing which plants to include in this handbook was a treacherous dilemma. So many of our treasured garden flowers are heirlooms. We could easily list all the wildflowers of the field and continue on for hundreds of pages—and we'd only be touching the tip of the iceberg. So we focused on the most commonly grown, easily recognizable heirlooms, leaving many gaps. Some of the plants you'll find in this book, however, are no longer commonplace.

While many once-valued plants have already been lost, preservationists have found many of the heirlooms described here by searching in obscure places and linking up with other gardeners. You, too, can help keep old-fashioned flowers alive by collecting seeds, growing vintage varieties of roses, sweet peas, phlox, or whatever happens to catch your fancy, and sharing seeds and plants with friends and family. Through our collective efforts, we can save our floral heritage from disappearing.

AN INTERVIEW
WITH SCOTT KUNST

CLASSIC BULBS

TOVAH MARTIN

SCOTT KUNST REFUSES to take a dewy-eyed approach to old-fashioned bulbs. Although the former school teacher now devotes all his time and energy to researching, collecting, and preserving heirloom bulbs, and providing them to the public through his mail-order catalog, Old House Gardens, he avoids romanticizing his mission. In his opinion, it's a flower's virtues that make it more valuable to gardeners over the long term than the myths and legends it has accrued along the way. "These are, simply, great garden plants," Scott explains. "They're tough, beautiful, distinctive, *and* they are freighted with the past.

"Heirloom bulbs are often tougher than their counterparts that have come and gone," says Scott. "That's one reason why they're still around. They can endure neglect, tough conditions, and a variety of climates. The same can be said for heirloom flowers in general. Have you ever wondered why *Hemerocallis fulva* can still be seen lining country roads? It endures because it's tough.

"Ninety-nine percent of their colleagues are gone," Scott says of the scores of bulbs that have slipped by the wayside, "but a handful of the best still remain." It's more than vigor that has kept a chosen few bulbs popular through the centuries, he points out. "It's often the unique individuals rather than the common, mainstream plants that have survived." One might call these botanical Babe Ruths. "Babe Ruth was one in a trillion. We've never found anyone else quite like him," Scott says. "It's the same with many heirlooms that have stood the test of time. They survive because their unique characteristics have not been duplicated." That's also what makes them so precious.

Scott illustrates his point with the 'Prince of Austria' tulip. "Introduced in 1860, it was sold as orange in the past, but today most

'Prince of Austria', introduced in 1860, is the most sweetly fragrant tulip.

people would call it red. Of course, there is nothing rare about a red tulip. But the fact is that 'Prince of Austria' is scented—it's the most sweetly fragrant tulip—and that virtue has kept it around." In fact, it was 'Prince of Austria' that launched Scott into the bulb-selling business. In 1990, when 'Prince of Austria' disappeared from the North American market, Scott felt compelled to take action, and so Old House Gardens in Ann Arbor, Michigan, was born.

Another unique heirloom, less endangered than 'Prince of Austria' but still hard to find today, is the hyacinth 'Distinction', which was introduced in 1880. "Its flowers are really too small to compete with its newer, larger colleagues," Scott says. "But no modern variety can match its deep maroon color and that attribute has saved it. The shade has been described as beet root, and it runs against the stereotype. There's nothing ho-hum about that hyacinth."

SUBTLE VIRTUES

Sometimes, a bulb's unique quality might not strike you as a virtue at first. Take *Crocus vernus* 'Grand Maître' from the 1920s. "It may seem like just another purple crocus," says Scott, "but it blossoms a bit later in the season—not what you would expect for a flower that's a classic

One of Scott Kunst's proudest "finds" is 'Semaphore', which he discovered at a family farm in France that has specialized in cannas for generations. Wildly popular among Victorian gardeners, cannas have been scorned for the past few decades.

harbinger of spring. 'Grand Maître' overlaps in bloom with the earliest daffodils—beautifully. It's got that special gift, and that's one reason why it's still here."

The special gifts that heirlooms possess are not necessarily the qualities that garden centers or flower-show exhibitors value. "Heirloom bulbs often have a wildflower look to them. They're more graceful and subtle than many modern bulb flowers," explains Scott. "Take the poet's narcissus, for example. *Narcissus poeticus*, pictured in the English herbals of the 1600s, grows wild in alpine meadows. It has more grace and delicacy than most modern daffodils. 'Tête-à-tête' daffodils are terrific in their own way, but their flowers always look to me like they're made of wax.

"Most older daffodils are willowy, graceful. Their flowers bounce in the breeze like butterflies in the garden," he says. "Their petals may be narrower, their cups smaller, their colors less intense—no blazing oranges, for example. But there's something ethereal about them."

Fragrance is often more pronounced in older varieties, too. "Fragrance today is way down on the list of garden virtues, perhaps because it isn't readily apparent in a picture. And it's hard to breed for. At one time, though, a flower without fragrance was considered lacking." Scott points out that "fragrance can still add an exciting dimension to a garden."

Victorian gardeners, including Monet and Gertrude Jekyll, loved gladiolii, which have since fallen out of fashion. Scott Kunst is working with the North American Gladiolus Council to try to find the oldest varieties. At right is 'Atom'.

Among old bulbs, there is often more diversity. The very old 'Duc van Thol' tulip, which dates back to 1620, blooms so early that you can combine it with hyacinths. Other old tulips have unusually long pointed petals, or colors in odd, soft "art shades." 'Zomerschoon' is one of the tulips traded for fortunes during the Dutch Tulipomania. Its tapestry of strawberry shades on a cream background put crude modern 'Rembrandts' to shame.

EVERYTHING COMES AND GOES

Scott is quite aware that fashion is alive and well in the garden. "Style changes in the garden just as it does in clothing or architecture," he says. "There are times when bell-bottoms are popular, and then there are times when bell-bottoms are totally passé. Attitudes change. There were times in this century when Victorian houses with all their gingerbread were considered to be in incredibly bad taste, but now we love them again."

How does that translate to bulbs? In the floral realm, cannas have been punted back and forth. Imported from subtropical America into Europe in the 1500s, cannas received a hero's welcome, reaching their zenith when the Victorian bedding pattern was king. Valued for their statuesqueness as well as their handsome foliage and vibrant flowers, cannas made a perfect bull's eye at the center of circular beds surrounded by rings of equally brilliantly colored annuals. But they were sacrificed in a blink of the eye when annual gardens were superceded by the pastel perennial border. "Cannas have been scorned for the last few decades," Scott says, "but the British garden guru Christopher Lloyd and many others are now re-popularizing them. Their time is clearly coming again."

When that time comes, Scott Kunst will be ready. One of his proudest "finds" is 'Semaphore', which he tracked down in France to a family farm that has specialized in cannas for generations. He describes it as having "narrow bronze leaves, and slender flowers a radiant, golden saffron orange."

Cannas are not the only bulbs that have suffered the buffeting of fashion; many other once-popular flowers are out of fashion at the moment. For the last 40 or so years, gladioli have suffered from a stigma, possibly because they were too often found in funeral arrangements. But, according to Scott, "the first hybrid glads were created in 1837, and Victorian gardeners—including Monet and Gertrude Jekyll—loved them. Sadly, of the thousands that have been introduced since then, the oldest survivors in North America date only to the 1920s to 1940s." He is currently working with the Old Timers Guild of the North American Gladiolus Council to remedy the situation.

THE ENTHUSIAST NETWORK

Where does Scott Kunst find his older varieties? A good route is via other collectors. One of his most fruitful friendships has been with the holder of the National Collection of hyacinths in Britain. Once a potato farmer, his life is now devoted to hyacinths. He's in contact with a collector in Latvia who has many hyacinths long lost in the Netherlands. And so it goes, one enthusiast helping another.

As Scott Kunst sees it, one advantage of Old House Gardens is that it is a small company. "I can offer a variety when only a hundred bulbs are available; larger companies must have much more stock." And so he is able to get rare bulbs to other gardeners who value their special qualities, ensuring that those varieties will not disappear despite mass-market pressures and the swings of fashion. "I hate to see a great old variety go extinct," he says. "They'll linger somewhere in the alleyways, you can be sure. But they belong in our gardens. They're amazing."

A COMPILATION OF CLASSIC BULBS

TOVAH MARTIN AND SCOTT KUNST

'King of the Striped', a Dutch crocus, has been traced back to 1880.

CROCUS

Native from Spain to Afghanistan, *Crocus vernus* was introduced into Europe by Clusius at the end of the 15th century. By the 1600s, the early herbalists Gerard, Besler, and Parkinson documented white, purple, and striped forms of the plant that we've come to know as "Dutch crocus." By the Victorian era, *Crocus vernus* had reached such a zenith of popularity that entire carpet-beds were devoted solely to the flowers in spring. Meanwhile, gardeners forced them indoors for winter entertainment. *Crocus vernus* 'Purpureus Grandiflora', introduced in 1870 and boasting rich purple blossoms, is the oldest purple Dutch crocus still available commercially. In the early 1900s species crocus gained a following with the popularization of the golden yellow *Crocus angustifolius* 'Cloth of Gold'. It was followed by several species such as *Crocus chrysanthus* 'Snowbunting' (1914) and *C. chrysanthus* 'Zwanenburg Bronze' (1931). Species crocus are smaller and more discreet than their Dutch counterparts, but they blossom several weeks earlier in the spring. For that virtue, they've earned the nickname "snow crocus."

FRITILLARIA
Crown imperials are native to southern Turkey, and first appeared in cultivation in Vienna in 1576. From Vienna they traveled to Holland and then, rather rapidly, to Britain, where the herbalist John Gerard already had "great plenty" by 1597. Held atop three-foot spikes, the flowers are big, brightly colored, and tulip-shaped, and nod downward. They're quite a sight. Early crown imperials, *Fritillaria imperialis*, were orange. However, a bright yellow version, 'Lutea', was introduced in 1665. According to Scott Kunst, 'Lutea' was considered a rarity in America in 1739.

GALANTHUS
Some historians claim that snowdrops are native to Britain; others feel that *Galanthus nivalis* arrived from Italy in the 15th century. Nicknamed because they blossom very early in the spring, when their grass-like leaves jut up above the melting snow, snowdrops have small, pure white, nodding blossoms with green markings. The fragrance is delightful. St. Francis is said to have embraced snowdrops as an emblem of hope; the early herbalist Gerard thought they were related to violets. At present, several variations of the species are readily available.

HYACINTHUS
Native to Turkey, Syria, and Lebanon, *Hyacinthus orientalis* was worn as a headdress by bridesmaids in Greek weddings and was mentioned in Homer's *Iliad*. However, the sturdy plants with thick spikes of inflated flowers didn't arrive in Europe until 1560. Although the Elizabethans found the intense aroma "melancholic," double white, blue, and pink varieties were available by 1613. Apparently, their esteem increased quickly so that by 1730, 2,000 hyacinths were in cultivation. When the Victorians began forcing bulbs in the mid-1800s, hyacinth popularity soared propitiously. The bulbs were also employed in 19th-century carpet-bedding patterns. In fact, according to Scott Kunst, the D. M. Ferry catalog of 1886 listed more hyacinths than tulips or daffodils.

MUSCARI
The grape hyacinth that we now call *Muscari botryoides* was originally grown as *Hyacinthus botryoides* and was in cultivation by 1576, originally collected from Spain. It is named for the grape-like clusters of deep purple flow-

The Elizabethans found the intense fragrance of hyacinths "melancholic," but the bulbs soared in popularity when the Victorians began forcing them and growing them in carpet-bedding patterns.

ers. The ancient herbalists, however, seemed dispassionate about the color. In fact, Parkinson seemed to prefer the white 'Album' form.

NARCISSUS

Several members of the narcissus family figured strongly in history, the first being *Narcissus tazetta*, grown by the ancient Greeks. Valued for its multi-headed bunches of small yellow and orange, fragrant blossoms, it is not reliably hardy but later became popular for forcing. By the 1880s, *N. tazetta* var. *orientalis*, also known as the Chinese sacred lily or Lien Chu lily, won the hearts of bulb-forcing Victorians. As for narcissi used outdoors, *N. poeticus*, the pheasant's eye narcissus, was mentioned by Theophrastus in 320 B.C.; however, the original form does not seem to have survived. The most commonly sold *N. poeticus* hybrid, often billed as "Old Pheasant's Eye," is actually a fairly recent hybrid known as 'Actaea', dating only to 1927, according to Scott Kunst. Daffodils were grown in English gardens as early as the 1500s, but they didn't enjoy great popularity until the 1860s, when the first hybrids became available. The famous, bright yellow 'King Alfred' first appeared in 1899. The cultivar now available by that name is actually a beefed-up version of the original.

Left: 'Flore Pleno' double snowdrop. Right: 'Barrii Conspicuus' narcissus.

TULIPS

Tulips were cultivated and coveted in the Middle East in the 12th and 13th centuries, but they weren't grown commercially in Europe until the mid-1500s. By the time the herbalist John Gerard wrote about the bulbs in 1597, seven types were available, including a red, a yellow, and a streaked variety. A virus spread by aphids caused the famous striped, streaked, and feathered "Rembrandt" tulips and also instigated the famous Dutch "Tulipomania" craze. Not only gardeners were bemused by the exotic coloration of the tulips; businessmen as well invested heavily in tulip speculation, and the bulbs became a hot trading commodity for reasons totally non-horticultural. Eventually, the tulip market collapsed and the virus weakened the strain so that few Rembrandts survive today. Scott Kunst has managed to make available 'Lac van Rijn' (1620), with red pointed petals and white edging, and 'Zomerschoon' (also 1620), with ivory petals flamed in red—both preserved by the Dutch national bulb museum. Frilly-petalled parrot tulips date to the 1600s. The earliest still available is 'Fantasy' (1910), with pink petals and apple-green markings. Darwin tulips, which were developed from antique Flemish varieties, became popular in the early 20th century.

Double pink 'Peach Blossom', a lush High Victorian tulip.

OLD GARDEN ROSES

TOVAH MARTIN

PETER SCHNEIDER DIDN'T get into old roses in the traditional way. "I sort of entered through the back door," he says. "Back in the early 1980s, I became interested in exhibiting flowers—I like to win prizes, you see. And no one in my region was growing or exhibiting heirloom roses. There were trophies just going begging. So that was my point of entry."

Together with his wife, Susan, Peter now runs Freedom Gardens in Freedom Township, Ohio, about an hour from Cleveland. He also edits *American Rose Rambler*, a bimonthly rose-related newsletter, and collects, imports, and exhibits roses. Now he not only takes home many prizes, but as an accredited rose judge, he also grants them.

Although he chuckles when he says that his original introduction to old roses was "totally mercenary," it didn't take long before the relationship became more meaningful. "I began to enjoy them for their own merits," he explains. "As the roses I planted for exhibition developed into mature plants, they didn't require the same care that modern roses needed. And they were hardier, especially the Albas, Damasks, and Gallicas. Every year, my modern roses died back to the ground, but the older roses were gaining size." Those virtues were the deciding factors in what became an ardent love affair.

Now Peter has five acres of rose gardens, with an emphasis on old roses. And he finds that his life is easier than when he focused on modern hybrids. Caring for the garden is not so arduous—but he emphasizes that not *all* old roses are carefree. To make his rose maintenance simpler, Peter avoids China and Tea roses, "which are not suited to the

Rosa sericea pteracantha, with its translucent red prickles (thorns), is one of Peter Schneider's favorite species roses.

Midwest and are prone to black spot." He also steers away from the Hybrid Perpetuals. "They're the endpoint of the old roses and are prone to disease. They were bred for exhibitors rather than gardeners," he says.

DAWN OF THE ROSE GARDEN

It was the Hybrid Perpetuals that helped change the look of our gardens. "Albas and Damasks were grown in the perennial border, among other flowers," Peter says. With the creation of the Hybrid Perpetual group, the rose garden was inaugurated, according to Peter. This separate place was set aside for roses raised specifically for cutting. "The original rose gardens were placed where people would not visit them often," says Peter, "because Hybrid Perpetuals aren't very attractive when they're not in blossom."

Hybrid Perpetuals also inspired a flurry of breeding. "The 1870s and 1880s were the Glory Days of Roses," Peter explains. "Thousands of roses appeared during those decades." The sudden proliferation came rapidly on the heels of a new understanding of rose breeding. "Before that time, gardeners selected plants for the characteristics they preferred. In the 1860s, Henry Bennett, a British cattle breeder, took the lessons that he'd learned from breeding animals and applied them to plants. He was the first to understand the importance of pollen." The knowledge that members of the same species could be bred with one another by transferring pollen between flowers led to experiments in genetics. With time, rose breeders were busily dusting the pollen from one flower onto the pistils of another blossom, working toward a particular goal. Perhaps they strove to combine the fragrance of the pollen parent with the color or form of the seed parent. Or perhaps they were trying to produce a bigger, longer-lasting blossom. As a result, the roster of roses burgeoned.

Hybrid Perpetuals were the beginning of the end for the old roses; they were particularly affected by the work of rose breeders. Gardeners found that the Hybrid Perpetuals remedied some of the pitfalls of the old varieties—they extended the blooming season, for example—but this

A ROSE GLOSSARY

ALBAS—Usually associated with the 18th century, these fragrant bloomers are known as the "white roses," although they also appear in delicate shades of pink.

CHINAS—Introduced into Europe at the end of the 18th century and not as hardy as previous roses, this class had one primary advantage—it blossomed repeatedly throughout the season.

DAMASKS—Probably the most ancient garden roses and brought into Europe from the Near East with the crusaders, these were cherished for their intense perfume and grown in monasteries during the Middle Ages.

DAVID AUSTIN HYBRIDS—Known as English Roses, this group was created by British rose breeder David Austin. A result of crossing old roses with modern Hybrid Teas and Floribundas, the group typically features shrubby growth, strong aroma, repeat flowering, and large, many-petalled flowers.

GALLICAS—One of the most ancient roses, also known as the Apothecary Rose, the French Rose, and the Red Rose. The color range is rich and varied and the group is very hardy.

group came with its own set of problems. "They require as much care as Hybrid Teas," says Peter. "They prefer leaf mold or rotted manure under foot and they need to be heavily fed"—one-half cup of 12-12-12 once a month, the same diet Peter gives his Hybrid Teas.

THE UPS AND DOWNS OF HEIRLOOMS

Old roses require varying degrees of care. "You can't expect to ignore any old rose and have it perform to its utmost," says Peter. Those that need the least maintenance are the Albas. "You just cut out the old wood to keep them shapely," he advises. And the ancient species roses are also not fussy. "On the opposite end of the care spectrum are the Hybrid Perpetuals; and the Damasks and Gallicas fall somewhere in between."

There are other traits that will inspire either love or hatred for heir-

---

HYBRID PERPETUALS—Created when Bourbon roses and Portland roses were crossed with Teas, Hybrid Perpetuals first appeared in France in the mid-19th century and boast good repeat blooms but are not reliably hardy.

HYBRID TEAS—The most popular roses in the 20th century, these are called "large-flowered bush roses" by the Rose Society. The result of crossing the Hybrid Perpetuals with Tea roses, they have impressive blossoms throughout the season.

MOSSES—First discovered in the early 18th century, Moss roses have lacy green bristles on the stems, calyxes, and sepals that give the appearance of moss.

PORTLANDS—Also known as the Damask Perpetuals and thought to have originated in Italy, from whence they came to France, the Portlands are among the parents of the Hybrid Perpetuals. They are extremely winter hardy and give excellent repeat bloom.

TEAS—First introduced in 1835, Teas were the result of crossing two of the original Chinas with Bourbons and Noisette roses. They are not reliably hardy outdoors.

Old garden roses require varying degrees of care. Those that require the least maintenance are the Albas. Above: 'Alba Semi-plena'.

PETER SCHNEIDER'S
FAVORITE OLD ROSES

These have performed best in his Zone 5 garden:

HYBRID PERPETUALS
- 'Baronne Prévost'
- 'Marchesa Boccella'

ALBAS
- "There's not an Alba that I don't like," he says, but at the top of his list are:
- 'Félicité Parmentier'
- 'Alba Semi-plena'

DAMASKS
- 'Madame Hardy'
- 'La Ville de Bruxelles'

MOSSES
- 'Crested Moss' (also known as 'Chapeau de Napoleon')

SPECIES
- *Rosa xanthina*—the first rose to bloom in spring, opening yellow
- *Rosa virginiana*—a late bloomer, a single medium pink
- *Rosa sericea*—grown for the translucent red thorns that ring its stem

loom roses. "If people shy away from old roses, it's for two main reasons," he says. "They don't repeat bloom and they're large for a typical suburban backyard." However, "the old roses that don't repeat give you twice as many flowers, all at once." As for their girth, it *can* be a stumbling block in a small yard. "I used to live on a 40-by-150-foot city lot, and I could only grow a limited number of old roses," he admits. "They're not all suitable for small gardens, and cutting them back curtails the bloom. You have to let them be what they want to be."

With nearly 20 years of old roses under his belt, Peter has come to know their eccentricities. Albas and Gallicas, much like apples, require a certain number of hours below freezing to set buds. In addition, the Gallicas, which are famed for their festive colors, must have cool weather when their buds are opening or the hues will be muddy rather than brilliant.

Peter has tried most of the vaunted remedies for black spot—a disease to which roses in general are susceptible—including the latest fad, spraying the bushes with fermented salmon manufactured by a company called Coast of Maine. "It was originally developed for deer prevention. But then gardeners began to find that it prevented black spot as well." While the recommended dilution is eight ounces per gallon of water, this strong solution can clog the sprayer. "And the smell is bound to bother the neighbors," Peter adds.

Baking soda and Sunspray, an ultrafine horticultural oil, is another frequently advised remedy for mildew. "Originally, it was supposed to work for black spot and mildew, but most people have found that it's really only effective for mildew," Peter says. "But it's not a cure-all," he cautions. "I find that the spray leaves spots that are just as unsightly as the mildew they're remedying."

Mildew is a problem with old as well as modern roses. "Any rose that is purple or mauve tends to get mildew," Peter has found. Unfortunately, the trait for fragrance is also linked to a tendency to get mildew. Both Gallicas and Hybrid Perpetuals are prone to mildew. "'Roger Lambelin' (1890) has very unique red petals with a white picotee edge, and it's extremely susceptible to mildew," Peter notes.

Peter Schneider isn't fanatical about old roses. He tries to keep an open mind. One group of modern roses that compares favorably, he believes, are the David Austin hybrids. "The Austin hybrids are similar to the Portland roses. But they have one major bonus—many Austin hybrids blossom in a color range that includes the apricots, coppers, and oranges. None of those colors existed in the European old roses."

One group of modern roses that compares favorably to the old roses is the David Austin hybrids, which are similar to the Portlands but blossom in a range of colors, including apricots and coppers. Below: 'Graham Thomas'.

AN ENCYCLOPEDIA OF OLD GARDEN ROSES

BEV DOBSON

THE DAMASKS

The Damasks are probably the most ancient garden roses of the Western Hemisphere. During the Crusades, they were carried to the western reaches of Europe from the Near East (not necessarily through the city of Damascus). In Europe, they were selected over the centuries for higher petal counts, repeat blooming, and fragrance. Damasks were cherished, grown, and protected, especially in the monasteries that sprang up in Europe during the Middle Ages. And nurturing was a crucial factor, because unlike the Gallicas, which sucker and form clumps if left on their own, the Damasks require cultivation.

Damask roses form thorny, untidy plants, throwing out a long cane here and there. Some are lax and tend to lie on the ground in a heap. Careful pruning alleviates both these problems in a garden situation, and staking or some sort of support such as a small trellis will also help tame them. Often, the blooms come three to a stem at once in an appealing conformation, with smaller blooms opening beneath the large main flower. Their fragrance is wonderful.

'Celsiana' is the cultivar I would recommend first of all. Pink with gold stamens, it is semi-double and makes a good, upright plant. The poise of the flowers on the stem is lovely and the fragrance is outstanding.

R. × *damascena* and *R.* × *damascena* var. *semperflorens*, the summer-flowering and the autumn damasks, are a lovely, even shade of pink. The rose hips are long and tubular and add greatly to winter-garden pleasure.

'Leda', formerly called 'The Painted Damask', produces red-stained buds that open to white blooms with some red edging showing.

'York and Lancaster' (*R.* × *damascena* 'Versicolor') is typical of the class but is considered an oddity due to its parti-colored blooms,

The semi-double 'Celsiana' is a Damask with outstanding fragrance.

with pink petals and some white in the same flower.

There are a few Damask Mosses that repeat-bloom. Those I have grown were in no way as fine as the Centifolia Moss roses, and to my mind the repeat was not a good enough trade-off. The Damask Perpetuals, also known as Portland roses, are another matter entirely and I consider them to be real treasures.

THE GALLICAS

Among the most ancient of roses, *R. gallica* 'Officinalis' was known as the Apothecary Rose, the French Rose, the Red Rose, and wrongly, the Red Damask. Its deep pink color was the closest to red of any of the roses of the Western Hemisphere. Its petals were not as fragrant as those of the Damask roses, but their redolence remained and intensified when they were dried.

Most of the Gallica roses form short, upright, compact clumps. They will sucker unless budded onto an understock, but tend to do this slowly. Flowers are held upright, beautifully poised on the plants, with a color range that is rich and varied. Foliage is neat but rough, not leathery or glossy; the plants are fairly thorny. Hips are decorative but not spectacular.

Gallicas are reputed to suffer in warm climates but are certainly very hardy in cold-winter areas, where they are suitable for herb gardens and small formal rose gardens. In mild climates, they make much larger plants than

Rosa gallica 'Officinalis', the Apothecary Rose, is one of the most ancient roses.

when stressed, and sucker more readily.

'Rosa Mundi', the striped sport of *R. gallica* 'Officinalis', is the most ancient and perhaps the most spectacular of all the striped roses.

'Tuscany' is one of the most velvety; it is lit with golden stamens, which are not quite so readily noticeable in the variety 'Tuscany Superb' (also known as 'Superb Tuscan').

'Cardinal de Richelieu'(1840) is another very deep-toned Gallica showing China influence in the foliage, which is paler green than that of most of its brethren.

'Charles de Mills' (alias 'Bizarre Triomphant'), also introduced in 1840, is full petalled, richly colored, and deep mauve-pink.

'Belle de Crécy' (1829) has pink, aging to mauve, flowers.

Marbled or spotted roses were popular in the first half of the 19th century but are rare now. 'Alain Blanchard' is the most readily available, with a sort of dotted appearance.

'Jenny Duval' shows a changing in color of petals from pink to deeper pink to mauve.

'Président de Sèze' displays a deeper mauve in the center with lighter or whitish mauve outer petals.

THE ALBAS

Called the "White Roses," though their perfumed flowers come in all the delicate shades of pink as well as white, most of the Albas are tall, upright plants with bluish green foliage. They are believed to have originated from a natural cross, and it has been suggested that this cross may have been between *R. canina* and *R. × damascena*. Conservative rosarians date the Albas to the 18th century, although there is some speculation that 'Maiden's Blush' actually pre-dates the 15th century.

Having grown and observed the Albas closely for more than 25 years, I find that the flowers are, without fail, perfectly symmetrical. They might be full and evenly petalled, with a "button center," or with a "confused center" (as in 'Maiden's Blush'). But they're all perfect. Anything more exquisitely beautiful would be hard to imagine.

All of the Albas cut well, last in bouquets, and do well in shows, with their strong stems. Every summer, I try to figure out how to describe the fragrance of the Albas, without success. It varies slightly with each different Alba variety, but is also unlike the scent of a Damask, Centifolia, or Gallica. The aromas are like carefully blended perfumes, I guess.

'Königin von Dänemark' has the deepest pink center of all the Albas. The color shows in the button eye, and very often the surrounding petals are "quartered," which means evenly divided, more usually in five parts than in four, but occasionally into three sections. It makes a dense, upright bush.

'Belle Amour' is an even, light pink, almost like a camellia.

Called the "White Roses," Albas come in shades of pink as well as white. 'Königin von Dänemark' is one of the pinkest.

'Madame Legras de Saint Germain' has sparkling white flowers with a yellow tint in the centers, most noticeable on overcast days.

'Maxima' is, as the name suggests, very full and pure white.

'Félicité Parmentier' is pale pink and makes a short, rounded bush.

THE CENTIFOLIAS

The Centifolias are also known as Provence roses, named for that region of southern France, though they are believed to have been developed by Dutch nurserymen. However, the Centifolias of today are thought to have no connection with the "hundred-leaved" (or actually, hundred-petalled) flowers of very ancient times.

Centifolias are very full-petalled blooms, usually evenly colored in shades of pink or white, rarely in deeper tones. The plants are mostly rather scraggly and are quite thorny. As a class, they present some interesting variations such as *R.* × *centifolia* 'Bullata', the lettuce-leaved rose, the miniature or dwarf Centifolias (such as 'Rose de Meaux' and 'Burgundian Rose'), the moss rose, and 'Crested Rose', which is a parallel sport and should not be lumped in with moss roses.

Centifolias tend to hold incurving petals until, as they age, the outer petals roll back, forming a "cup and saucer" appearance. You will find them in many old flower paintings and painted on china.

The Victorians were fond of curiosities, such as roses with mossy-looking resin-secreting glands on their stems, calyxes, and sepals.

Moss roses such as 'Gloire des Mousseuses' were the most typical roses of the Victorian period.

Because they become such unkempt-looking plants, and throw unmanageably wild canes with such thorny stems and nodding flowers, it's easy to understand why they came to be superceded. But we are fortunate indeed that so many have come down to us.

R. × *centifolia* 'Variegata' is a well-formed, upright, even, dense bush, lovely in every way.

'La Noblesse' is scraggly, but worth pruning and staking because of its fragrant and evenly formed flowers, although most of those blossoms are held on nodding stems.

THE MOSS ROSES

Botanically speaking, roses do not have thorns—they have prickles, bristles, hairs, glands, and pubescence. In Moss roses, resin-secreting glands occur on the stems, calyxes, and sepals, giving them a mossy appearance and a piney fragrance. This trait was first discovered in the 17th century or early in the 18th century. And by the end of the first quarter of the 18th century, Moss roses were introduced into commerce and continued to be popular through the mid-19th century and beyond. It has been suggested that Moss roses were the most typical roses of the Victorian age.

'Gloire des Mousseuses' is a sport of the Centifolias with clear, bright pink flowers.

'William Lobb' is known as the Old Velvet Moss, with deep-toned flowers.

THE BOURBONS

On the Île de Bourbon (near Réunion), where farmers divided their fields with hedges of China and Damask roses, Monsieur Perichon found among the young plants one that was very different from its neighbors and he planted it in his garden. In 1817, Monsieur Bréon, on botanical travels for the Government of France, saw it and sent seeds to the gardener of the Duc d'Orléans at the Château de Neuilly near Paris. By 1823, sufficient stock was built up so that the rose was available to French rosarians, and thus the Bourbon class of roses got its start.

'Souvenir de la Malmaison' may have been the most famous of the Bourbons, which peaked in popularity between 1830 and 1870.

That's one version of the story, but it's not the entire truth. A Bourbon rose also appeared on the island of Mauritius and was sent to the Luxembourg Gardens in Paris in 1821. And it also existed in the Calcutta Botanical Garden under the name 'Rose Edouard', and was widely used in India as an understock. Whether the same natural cross happened in the fields in more than one place, or whether the rose was simply transported (there were sea routes between the places of possible origin and the Cape of Good Hope), is a fact lost to history.

The Bourbons were most popular as garden roses from 1830 to 1870. Some do not have a strong early bloom, but are fine fall bloomers. Few roses in any class can compete with Bourbons for wonderful color, wide, silky petals, and intense fragrance. They are noble garden plants, though some benefit from a low trellis or staking.

'Souvenir de la Malmaison' may be the most famous of the Bourbons and has many fans (although Vita Sackville-West was not among them). There is both a bush form and a climber.

'Zéphirine Drouhin' may also claim "most popular" status: It's a thornless climber in a rather strong pink.

'La Reine Victoria' has dusky pink flowers on a tall and slender but upright standing shrub. Its sport, 'Madame Pierre Oger', is a paler pink.

'Commandant Beaurepaire' is a spectacular striped variety and makes a good bush with lovely, rather light green foliage.

THE PORTLANDS

The Portlands are the Damask Perpetuals that, together with the Bourbons, melted in with Chinas and Teas to produce the Hybrid Perpetuals. Little is known of their past, except that they are thought to have originated in Italy and traveled to France. A supposed connection with the Duchess of Portland gave them their class name.

William Paul listed 84 Portlands in his 1838 catalog. But today we have only four or five, depending on how you class certain varieties. They repeat well even without careful pruning and make neat, upright, rounded bushes that are suitable for the small garden.

I think it is fair to say that the Portlands are under-appreciated. They are especially valuable for gardens in severe winter climates, where they should be tried. They will probably be entirely winter hardy and give better repeat bloom than most other hardy roses.

I consider the Portlands suitable, along with the Gallicas, for the herb garden, by virtue of their fragrance and also because they repeat bloom (unlike the Gallicas), and because they provide architectural solidity in plant form. They are also good in other parts of a garden.

'Comte de Chambord' and 'Jacques Cartier' (also known as 'Marquise Bocella') have full pink blooms forming "powder puffs" of more than 300 petals.

'Rose du Roi' blossoms in deep tones of red bordering on purple.

'Rose de Rescht' has very deep pink blossoms.

THE HYBRID PERPETUALS

The French name for the class, Hybrid Remontants ("repeat blooming"), would be a more descriptive title for the Hybrid Perpetual class. Most of them were raised in France, though they became the foundation of the British rose show. They fit into three distinct groups: The earliest are very close to the old-fashioned form; those in the middle section are equally full petalled but larger and globular—what people think of as "cabbage roses" fit into this group; and members of the third group resemble the Hybrid Teas very closely.

The class began when the Bourbons and Damask Perpetuals (the Portlands) crossed with Teas. Hybrid Perpetuals tend to have strong, upright, thornless or nearly thornless branches, with fragrant blooms supported by good stems. They must be pruned to produce good repeat bloom and require lots of fertilizer and water. They are spectacular show blooms but many varieties proved disappointing as garden roses, to the point that they were considered suitable only for the conservatory.

'Baronne Prévost' is an example of the first group of Hybrid Perpetuals, blossoming in rich, medium pink. Introduced in 1842, it is very full petalled with a button center and, unlike many in the class, is rather thorny.

'Mrs. John Laing', introduced in 1887 by Henry Bennett, was once widely planted, if not over-planted, in this country. It is a lovely cool pink with a hint of lavender.

'Ferdinand Pichard' is a particularly good striped variety and belongs in every collection of Hybrid Perpetuals.

'Frau Karl Druschki' is a superb white rose, sometimes showing a flush of pink on an outer petal. Sadly, there is no fragrance.

'Victor Verdier', introduced in 1859, blossoms in deep pink and might reasonably be considered the first Hybrid Tea.

'Mrs. John Laing', a Hybrid Perpetual, was introduced in 1887 and widely planted in the United States. Hybrid Perpetuals are good repeat bloomers if pruned and fertilized, and tend to be fragrant.

AN INTERVIEW WITH CHRISTIE WHITE

VINTAGE CLIMBERS

TOVAH MARTIN

LONG BEFORE SHE BECAME Program Coordinator for Horticulture at Old Sturbridge Village, an outdoor museum of early New England history in Sturbridge, Massachusetts, Christie White began her romance with vines. Asked to trace the origins of this affection, she slips back to her childhood, when weekends were spent visiting her maternal grandfather's garden in the small mill town of Uxbridge, Massachusetts. "It was grandfather's custom to show things off; he just loved to brag. Every weekend, we got the tour of his shiny, heavily waxed car, his impeccable house, and his incredible garden." Christie gained from the experience. "You entered the garden through a seated arbor. It was quite a fantasy for a child," she recalls.

Beyond the arbor, the garden was filled with cottage bloomers such as hollyhocks and Canterbury bells. "Later I learned that those were traditional flowers, but they were all I knew at the time." Not only did Christie grow up with vintage flowers to the exclusion of the latest novelties, but she also was exposed to many of the age-old names for blossoms. "My grandmother never called *Viola tricolor*, Johnny jump-ups. They were "ladies' delight" to her. But she used one name that was probably unique to her: Cleomes were called electric-light plants in our family because the stamens reminded my grandmother of light-bulb filaments." It might not have been common usage, but the name was descriptive.

Christie did not stray far from her element when she went from studying English literature to being a costumed interpreter at Old Sturbridge Village. She started in the kitchen garden in 1981, and that was where her formal study of heirloom plants began. "What intrigues me is the connection between plants and people," Christie says. "I like

planning gardens that reinforce broader themes, like the closeness between humanity and nature."

ROMANTIC YET PRACTICAL

Her grandfather's garden not only promoted an early respect for traditional bloomers, but his

In the first half of the 19th century, vines such as grapes, which could boast multiple uses, were warmly welcomed into gardens still shaped by the principle of utilitarianism.

seated arbor also instilled in Christie a fondness for vines. Vines were an integral part of early American gardens. Christie finds repeated reference to vines in literature of the 1830s, the decade that Old Sturbridge Village depicts. "Seed catalogs and advice literature all support a real interest in vines—imported and native, annual and perennial. I see it as a prelude to the later 19th-century fascination for anything romantic.

"That decade was on the cusp between the 18th-century Age of Reason and the later Romantic Period," Christie theorizes, "and people were seesawing between the two. Before that time, gardens had a high degree of order. Vines were a way for Americans to ease themselves into a passionate garden."

When she lectures, which she does often, Christie liberally quotes from *The Young Florist*, a book written by Joseph Breck in 1833. The garden that the book describes captures the moment in the transition between formal and informal. Breck considered himself a champion of the country garden—to a degree. In his opinion, too many gardeners were being swayed by the vagaries of fashion or, as he put it, "the flickering meteor called taste." In *The Young Florist*, two children, a brother and sister, are faced with a 40-by-40-foot tract of land, and lay plans for a garden. The sister suggests romantic serpentine walkways and undulating beds. Her practical brother quells her dreams, explaining that if they had acres at their disposal, he could indulge her whims. But they have only a small plot, and so they must opt for strict geometry. "However," says Christie, "the brother suggests that they construct a rustic birch sapling arbor as the central focal point, leaving the twigs on the birch limbs to tie informally in a bower. Vines would be trained on that support." It was a nod in the direction of the foot-loose and fancy-free.

As far as Christie can figure, arbors and trellises originated in the practical realm of the kitchen garden, where peas and beans required support. But over time, these structures became more ornamental, supporting vines that were not purely functional. By the time *The Young Florist* was published in 1833, a full complement of

Arbors and trellises originated in the practical realm of the kitchen garden, where edible climbers required support. But over time, these structures began sporting the cypress vine and other ornamental plants.

vines was firmly established in the garden. Mentioned were nasturtiums (which have only recently been bred for clumpiness; previous types had trailing stems and were encouraged to ramble), scarlet cypress vine, balloon vine, love-in-a-puff, morning glories, and hyacinth beans. In addition, Christie has found that cobaea, passion flowers, sweet peas, scarlet runner beans, balsam apples, and balsam pears were also prevalent by the 1830s. The clock vine (*Thunbergia grandiflora*), just beginning its reign of popularity, was still considered a novelty. Among the hardy vines mentioned were the trumpet vine (*Campsis radicans*), Dutchman's pipe (*Aristolochia macrophylla*), Virgin's bower (*Clematis virginiana*), honeysuckles, and rambling roses (especially sweetbriars, valued for their fragrant leaves as well as flowers).

Although it lacked blossoms, English ivy was often employed for its all-encompassing and camouflaging verdure. And, most especially, Christie found that vines that could boast multiple uses, such as fruiting grapes, were most warmly welcomed into gardens still shaped by the principle of utilitarianism.

MODEST BUT EYE-CATCHING

Christie has noticed that our forefathers and mothers seemed quite content with blossoms that were small and discreet. "They liked to examine things closely, and so they weren't obsessed with larger blossoms. It's only relatively recently that flowers have had to be the size of dinner plates. A good example is the native clematis, which is overlooked in favor of those larger-than-life modern hybrids." Vines also possessed one feature that enhanced their modest virtues—they could be viewed easily at eye level. Even the smallest blossoms are in your face. Among other virtues, intriguing seed pods were considered a bonus.

Vines served several functions. There was the obvious employment: producing shade. Bowers were encouraged over seating and play areas. Vines also came in handy for camouflage. At first, Christie was confused by the terminology. "They spoke about masking offensive odors emanating from the 'offices' of the house. Turned out they were referring to the 'functional' buildings." The outhouses, that is.

But fragrant vines were not confined to merely deodorizing duties. Fragrance was much appreciated for its own sake. In fact, arbors were most often positioned in front of doorways where scents might float indoors. Windows flaunted trellises above their frames "like eyebrows," often covered with scented flowers to send gusts of perfume through open sashes. "People walked in their gardens; they applied their noses to blossoms," says Christie.

Fences in poor repair, ramshackle buildings, and naked walls—vines were appropriate and convenient for camouflaging anything unsightly. They were not, however, often used to cover the fences in front of a residence. Although most properties were fenced to keep wandering livestock from marauding in the garden, the fences also served a decorative function, especially in front of the house. Most early Americans did not hide the proud pickets that fronted "home sweet home."

Flowers in general, and vines in particular, were often seen as morally uplifting elements. And vines, because of their tendency to enwrap the structure, transformed a house into a thing of beauty. The residents inside could scarcely help but feel the beneficial impact.

And that brings us back to Christie's introduction to gardening. Although she has only a vague memory of the specific flowers that grew in the gardens of her childhood, something positive happened every time she passed through her grandfather's seated arbor.

Virgin's bower, *Clematis virginiana*, was grown by early Victorian gardeners, who liked to examine blossoms up close. The native clematis has since been eclipsed by larger-than-life modern hybrids.

A SELECTION OF
VINTAGE CLIMBERS

TOVAH MARTIN AND CHRISTIE WHITE

Aristolochia
DUTCHMAN'S PIPE

The name Dutchman's pipe refers to the uniquely curved shape of the blossoms produced on this rambling, all encompassing, heart-leaved vine. But the name birthwort describes the medicinal use of *Aristolochia macrophylla*. It was valued for the dense, cooling shade it cast—perfect for porches and gazebos—as well as its small but intriguing blooms. Welcomed as a curiosity in early American gardens, it is an obscure vine now, rarely cultivated.

Clematis
TRAVELER'S JOY

The first clematis to come into cultivation was *Clematis vitalba*, called traveler's joy by virtue of the shade it afforded anyone on a journey. Perhaps a little rampant for the modern garden, this species with tiny white, fragrant flowers from August to October served its purpose as a cover-up for outbuildings until recent times, when we put a premium on tidiness. Together with *C. viorna* and *C. flammula,* it was mentioned in many early

Dutchman's pipe was valued for its dense shade and curious flowers.

American catalogs. Equally popular was *C. viticella*, the first imported clematis to enter Britain. Known for its nodding, dusky rose blossoms, it was a favorite medicinal herb of Queen Elizabeth I. The first large-flowering, hybrid clematis—and the precursor of all the star-shaped, large-flowering vines that are grown so widely today—was the white-flowering 'Henryi', which is still on the market. Bred in 1855, it was the handiwork of Isaac Anderson-Henry of Edinburgh.

Cobaea
CUP AND SAUCER VINE
This Mexican native, discovered in 1789, is handsome even without its flowers. In addition to its deeply cut leaves with bronze undersides, and curly tendrils late in the season, its gaping, green trumpets that turn gradually to lilac and then dark purple make this a riveting plant.

Humulus lupulus
HOP VINE
The flowers of *Humulus lupulus* have been used in brewing since ancient times, and for this reason hops were banned in England in 1528 when the monarch wanted control of the beverage. By 1603, the law was rescinded, but hop production wasn't widespread in Britain until the end of the 17th century. Meanwhile, in 1648, hop vine had come to North America, where it was welcomed as a camouflage vine as well as for its use as a sleep-inducing tea, in brewing, and as a dried flower.

Cup and saucer vine, native to Mexico, is a riveting plant with deeply cut leaves and large green trumpets that turn lilac and then dark purple.

Ipomoea
MORNING GLORY

Native to tropical America, morning glories arrived in Britain in the 1620s, but they were too similar to the rampant nuisance bindweed, *Convolvulus arvensis,* to gain any sort of following in the cultivated garden. Furthermore, morning glories blossomed and closed too early in the morning (pre-dawn) and produced flowers too late in the season to become commercially successful. Until the current century, they were used primarily as foliage climbers to camouflage unsightly buildings. It wasn't until 1931, when an amateur gardener by the name of Clarke found in his field in Colorado a morning glory with sky-blue blossoms that tarried until noon and flowered by mid-summer that morning glories became popular. After 'Clarke's Early Heavenly Blue' hit the scene, all sorts of morning glories were introduced, including 'Blue Star', 'Flying Saucers', 'Wedding Bells', 'Candy Pink', and 'Summer Skies'. They were lost in the 1960s, deleted from catalogs, but there's been a recent effort to recollect and distribute them.

Lablab purpureus
HYACINTH BEAN
Formerly known as *Dolichos lablab*, the hyacinth bean is now called *Lablab purpureus*. Native to tropical Africa, it was introduced into Britain from India in 1794.

Top: 'Flying Saucers' morning glory.
Bottom: hyacinth bean.

Beloved for its brick-red seed pods and lilac-colored flowers, it was also valued for its edible beans, used like kidney beans.

Lathyrus
SWEET PEA
We have Father Cupani, a Franciscan monk, to thank for introducing the first sweet pea into Britain, in 1696. Not only was he attracted by the bi-colored, deep blue and purple blossoms, but also the incredibly aromatic perfume of the flowers. It's difficult to imagine that attraction given the faintly scented modern versions of sweet peas. 'Cupani', as it was called (and it has been reintroduced, thanks to the efforts of Peter Grayson of Derbyshire), emits an aroma reminiscent of honey and warm beeswax, poured forth even more heavily at dusk. Unfortunately, sweet peas lost their fragrance in 1900, when gardeners began to breed for larger, wavy-petaled blossoms on long stems, suitable for cut-flower work. Older hybrids, again available due to Peter Grayson's efforts, include 'Painted Lady' (1737), 'Prima Donna' (1896), 'Fairy Queen' (1873), 'Captain of the Blues' (1891), and 'Black Knight' (1898).

Lonicera sempervirens
HONEYSUCKLE
In his 1841 volume, the *American Flower Garden Directory,* Robert Buist called *Lonicera sempervirens,* the trumpet honeysuckle, "the most attractive object in all our country gardens." This vine, native from Connecticut to Florida, may have reigned supreme, but other honeysuckles were equally evident in early gardens—especially climbing on outbuildings where camouflage and sweet scent might come in handy. They belong to the Caprifoliaceae, a family whose botanical name refers to the plants' attractiveness to roaming goats.

Passiflora
PASSION FLOWER
The first passion flower to be presented to Europe was *Passiflora incarnata,* later known as the maypop. Originally welcomed with much ceremony as a miracle to help the South American missionaries illustrate the story of the passion, the maypop arrived in Britain in 1629 but didn't lend itself well to greenhouse cultivation. It performs much better in the ground and was hailed as among the garden's best vines by Buist in 1841. It was noted at the time that this vine died to the ground every winter but each year put forth shoots 20 to 40 feet long with palm-like leaves, and purple, interestingly filamented flowers. For potted, indoor cultivation, we now have *Passiflora × alato-caerulea* and *Passiflora caerulea.*

Opposite: In the mid 19th century, passion flowers were hailed as among the best vines for the garden.

AN INTERVIEW WITH PEGGY CORNETT

ANTIQUE ANNUALS

TOVAH MARTIN

GARDENING GOES WAY BACK in Peggy Cornett's family. Her grandfather tended a sizable orchard as well as a vegetable garden at his home in the South, and her mother followed suit, cultivating the vegetables that her in-laws had preserved at their Kentucky home. "Gardening was in my blood, I guess," Peggy figures.

But she didn't spend much time in the garden until her brother was killed in the Vietnam War. She was twelve years old. Before that moment, gardening had been a chore burdened by boring hours of endless weeding. But she spent the summer her brother died by her mother's side in the garden. "It was sort of a healing thing for her. That was the summer she told me about our family's heirloom pole beans, the ones that melt in your mouth like butter. And she showed me the differences between the other family beans as well, taking them in her hand and pointing out their unique shapes and how they were used in the family recipes. I have real strong memories of that summer."

That summer was Peggy's initiation into heirlooms. Although vegetables were her family's main focus, she learned about more than just beans. "I remember the French marigolds in the garden as well. My mother didn't waste much time on those marigolds; she was busy growing enough food to feed the family. Nevertheless, she always planted them, and she always planted nasturtiums as well."

No one was surprised when Peggy decided to study botany in college. The University of North Carolina at Chapel Hill had no horticulture program per se, so Peggy constructed her own syllabus. She worked with camellias and at the same time discovered a fascination for native plants. An undercurrent of interest in historic horticulture, though, was the motivation that drove her research. Although histori-

The whims of fashion have had a big impact on the history of annuals. For example, bright orange calendulas were more common in the 19th century than they are now.

ans had written about perennials, Peggy realized that the history of annuals was virtually neglected, so she began to explore the topic. She brought together what she gathered from primary sources—dusty volumes, catalogs, and periodicals housed at libraries, including the Pennsylvania Horticulture Society and the Massachusetts Horticultural Society—in a volume called *Popular Annuals of Eastern North America 1865-1914,* published in 1985 by Dumbarton Oaks.

WHERE HAVE ALL THE ANNUALS GONE?

Peggy not only explored what she calls "the premiere annuals" such as marigolds, zinnias, petunias, and pansies—plants that are still featured prominently in modern seed catalogs—but also discovered a roster of bygone annuals that failed to survive the test of time. To her surprise, the list of popular annuals has diminished rather than expanded over the years.

For example, every 19th-century catalog that she consulted featured *Abronia,* the sand verbena. "Native to California," she says, "they were funny little things that looked like verbenas blooming in

In the 19th century, Western natives such as sand verbena summoned romantic images of new territories and brave explorers. Many failed to endure as garden plants.

rosy lilac or yellow. Every catalog began its offerings with *Abronia,* and yet you never see it listed any longer." Likewise, collinsias fell out of favor. Peggy describes these members of the snapdragon family from California as free-blooming annuals "that looked like lupines from a distance."

Why did these plants fail to endure? Peggy surmises that, although the flowers seemed perfectly worthy at first glance when they were discovered thriving in their native habitat, they didn't adapt well to gardens. She uses the sand verbena as an example. "Sand verbena was described as growing in the most barren sand hills and on the boulders of the Pacific Coast within a few feet of high water." Initially, sand verbena made a big splash. But gradually, it was abandoned when it failed to perform up to expectations elsewhere. "Seed didn't germinate well, and the plants never looked vigorous when grown on the East Coast. The Victorians tried in vain to grow the sand verbena, but it eventually slipped out of fashion." The harsh terrain of the Pacific Coast yielded some beauties, but who could construct a similar ecosystem?

Several California natives suffered a similar fate. Many hit the scene, made a dramatic entry, then fell out of popularity just as rapidly. Others lingered for a while. "There was a fascination with anything from the West," Peggy points out. "The literature was peppered with

Some annuals —sweet peas, for example, not only endured but also thrived, giving birth to the American seed indus try. Right, sweet pea 'America'.

descriptions of the plants in the wild, and they were the stuff of daydreams, with images of brave new territories and romantic views of the Western expansion." The British were particularly keen on many of the annuals from the West. "*Gilia capitata* was introduced in 1833 and was highly esteemed in Britain by such garden experts as Jane Loudon, but never received a great deal of attention in the American trade," says Peggy.

ROMANTIC DISCOVERIES

Not all the newly introduced Westerners failed. One survivor is the California poppy (*Eschscholzia californica*), discovered by a Russian expedition in 1815 and named for the surgeon of the crew. The public warmed to romantic descriptions of discoveries. Peggy found this commentary on the initial sightings of California poppy in Harriet L. Keeler's *Our Garden Flowers,* written in 1810: "The early Spanish explorers sailing back and forth along the California coast noted the flame of the poppies along the hillsides coming down to the sea, and called the coast the Land of Fire." Burdened by a nearly unpronounceable (and definitely unspellable) botanical name, California poppy has nonetheless remained a premiere annual since 1860.

Discoveries were not confined to California. Drummond's phlox

(*Phlox drummondii*), hailing from Texas, was collected by Thomas Drummond in 1835. Available in a variety of colors with various forms and several heights from dwarf on up, Drummond's phlox took the gardening world by storm. However, it performed half-heartedly in gardens on the East Coast and eventually moved into the realm of relative unknowns.

Trends were not necessarily the same on both sides of the ocean. Clarkia, named for Captain Clark of the Lewis and Clark Expedition, piqued interest in England due to the similarities between the British climate and that of the Pacific Coast. Double varieties appeared, several color forms were on the European market, and clarkia became a prominent cut flower. However, it sulked in the hot, dry summers typical of North America and was virtually ignored in this country.

THE WHIMS OF FASHION

Color preferences also had an impact on the history of annuals. Bright orange calendulas were more common in the 19th century than they are at present. The gangly, informal amaranths were more popular when gardens were inhabited by tall, floppy plants rather than the carefully clipped annuals of the 20th century. Fashion is everything in the garden, and the tides of flowers ebb and flow according to its changing whims.

The trend in sweet peas was for increased flower size and spire length on more compact vines. In the process, fragrance was forfeited. Says Peggy: "A lot of people lamented the loss of fragrance, but sweet peas still fell victim. Similarly, the aroma of mignonettes was reduced when they developed the giant-flowered types. And the original species snapdragon has a fine fragrance; when they bred bigger-blossomed and bicolored snapdragons, the fragrance was diminished."

Fragrance was not the only characteristic to go by the wayside. The older nasturtiums were grown as climbers with foliage that crept hither and yon. This changed with the development of compact forms. One early dwarf nasturtium was known as the Variegated Leaved Queen or Tom Thumb Chameleon.

Other annuals fell victim to disease rather than fashion. China aster (*Callistephus chinensis*) was discovered by a Jesuit missionary in Peking in the early 1730s. It was embraced, improved by hybridizers, and was "considered indispensable in parterres and carpet beds," says Peggy. She quotes James Vick, a nurseryman and garden writer who commented in 1865 that "no class of flowers has been so much improved within the past twenty years as this splendid genus, and

The California poppy has remained popular. An 1810 garden book noted that early Spanish sailors, observing "the flame of the poppies along the hillsides coming down to the sea," called the California coast "the Land of Fire."

none has advanced so rapidly in popular favor. They are now as double as the chrysanthemum or the dahlias, and almost as large and showy as the peony, and constitute the principle adornment of our gardens during the autumn months." Eventually, China asters succumbed to aster yellow. However, resistant varieties are staging a comeback.

Some annuals have not only endured, but also thrived. Nasturtiums, zinnias, marigolds, sweet peas, pansies, snapdragons, and petunias have remained staples—so far. These annuals gave birth to and nurtured the seed industry in this country. Sweet peas, for example, are credited with creating a fertile market for American seed houses. According to Peggy, "Joseph Breck and Sons was one of the first American enterprises to recognize and import the improved sweet peas, but W. Atlee Burpee and Company soon became a leader in seed distribution. California became a seed production center during the 1890s, primarily through the seed farms of C. C. Morse and Company of San Francisco. It was at the Morse farms that the type of plant from which Burpee's Cupid sweet peas were derived was developed. Cupid was introduced by Burpee in 1893 as the first dwarf, white-flowered sweet pea."

Over the years, zinnias were much improved. "The original zinnia was a muddy pale lavender in color, first illustrated in *Curtis' Botanical Magazine* in the 1790s," Peggy points out. Many years ensued before steps were taken toward the flower's betterment. In 1908, she notes, James Vick commented that it hadn't been long since zinnia was considered a coarse plant; but by then giant-flowered as well as dwarf varieties were available.

Despite the successes stories, however, fewer and fewer of the old-fashioned annuals survive. Every plant on the current list of favorites was on the market a century ago; the difference, as Peggy points out, is that "we've reduced our selection drastically." Gone or rarely grown are the candytufts, mignonettes, Mexican prickly pears, catchflies, and love-lies-bleeding of yesteryear. They might make a comeback, but they are all but forgotten at present.

As Director of the Thomas Jefferson Center for Historic Plants, Peggy Cornett is striving to preserve the antique flowers that have been lost or nearly lost.

Drummond's phlox, a Texas native, took the early Victorian gardening world by storm, then moved into the realm of the relative unknowns.

THE BEST
ANTIQUE ANNUALS

TOVAH MARTIN

Amaranthus caudatus
LOVE-LIES-BLEEDING

Fashions come and go, especially in flowers. And, for a time—in the not-so-distant past—magenta was not permitted in the garden. Garden trendsetter Gertrude Jekyll banished magenta blooms from her garden and others followed her lead, possibly explaining the disappearance of love-lies-bleeding. Native to Peru, Africa, and India, *Amaranthus caudatus* was introduced before 1665, and was first called the "great purple flower-gentle." Its long, deep magenta catkins, dangling down from three- to four-foot-tall plants, were greatly admired in both Elizabethan and Victorian times. Interestingly, love-lies-bleeding can again be found at garden centers. Perhaps it is making a comeback.

Love-lies-bleeding.

Antirrhinum majus
SNAPDRAGON

By Elizabethan times, *Antirrhinum majus* was already available with flowers in purple, white, pink, red with a yellow throat, and red with yellow veins. Those original snapdragons, so beloved in the 17th century, stood three feet or taller and were scentless. In fact, it wasn't until 1963 that the first scented snapdragon appeared in commerce—a rare situation in horticulture; more often, blossoms lost scent with time. The first dwarf hybrid, 'Tom Thumb', didn't appear on the scene until the 1880s.

Callistephus chinensis
CHINA ASTER

Discovered by a Jesuit missionary in a field near Peking in the 1730s and originally thought to be an aster, the first *Callistephus* had single flowers with rows of purple ray petals. By 1750, the flower was already available in blue, white, red, and purple on top of ornamental, serrated leaves. Although popular until the mid 20th century, China asters are certainly not as ragingly popular as they once were, but are making a comeback. Although old forms are prone to aster yellows, new resistant forms are now on the market.

Celosia argentea var. *cristata*
COCKSCOMB

The first cockscomb to come into cultivation was the red, crested *Celosia argentea* var. *cristata* that arrived in Europe in 1570; the plumed and feathered types came later. Eighteenth-century gardeners, afraid to let anything that looked so rare mingle in the beds, grew cockscombs as potted plants. Early-20th-century gardeners continued to coddle cockscomb, proudly exhibiting at local fairs specimens with expansive crests.

Clarkia
CLARKIA

By the 1860s, two clarkias were already in cultivation, named for Captain Clark of the Lewis and Clark Expedition. Of those, it was

Top: China aster. Bottom: cockscomb.

Clarkia unguiculata, with its cup-shaped flowers made up of triangular, lavender-pink petals, that received the most attention and was soon available in a variety of bright colors. Alas, clarkias, native to the Pacific Coast, failed to thrive in the hot summers typical of the rest of the country. They soon slipped out of popularity throughout most of the country, but are still grown as a cut flower on the West Coast and in other cool-summer regions.

Consolida
LARKSPUR
Introduced into Britain from the Mediterranean in the mid-16th century, larkspurs were prevalent in gardens until relatively recently, when they were totally superceded by delphiniums. Nowadays it's difficult to find larkspur, although the slender spires of white-, pink-, or purple-spurred blossoms on top of a three foot stem of pencil-thin leaves are wonderful for weaving between other plants.

Cosmos
COSMOS
Cosmos was introduced into Britain from its native Mexico in 1799. Originally, cosmos was unlikely to set buds until a few weeks before it was smitten by frost throughout most of North America, and so it wasn't a common garden flower. In the early 20th century, though, the brightly colored flowers were bred to

Western natives, clarkias, including *Clarkia unguiculata,* were named after Captain Clark of the Lewis and Clark expedition.

Left: California poppy. Right: sunflowers.

bloom earlier in the summer. When that improvement came, cosmos was already available in white, pink, and deep red.

Eschscholzia
CALIFORNIA POPPY

One of the Pacific Coast species that has translated well in gardens throughout the country is the California poppy. First discovered by Spanish explorers sailing along the California coast in 1815, the California poppy varied widely in the wild. Other than the recent introduction of muted shades to tone down the uncompromising oranges typical of the species, it remains basically the same as the plant that 19th-century gardeners knew and loved.

Helianthus annuus
SUNFLOWER

The Spanish took the sunflower back to their country from South America in the 16th century, undoubtedly impressed by the big, brightly colored daisy so valued by the Incas. By that time the Native Americans had already selected many versions of *Helianthus annuus*—sunflowers with lots of branches and smaller flowers, or larger blooms on fewer branches, depending upon the regions in which they were being grown. Hopi Indians bred a purple-seeded variety for dyes and other tribes grew sunflowers for their oil-rich seeds or their meaty flower heads. Today, we are particularly fond of the mammoth version with one big flower balanced on a single stem.

Impatiens
BALSAM

By 1542, *Impatiens balsamina*, a recent introduction to Europe, was already widely grown. Before long, it was available in white, cream, pink, lilac, red, and crimson. Bicolored versions were available by 1706, and further innovations such as double, camellia-like balsams and striped types soon followed. All were immensely popular in early gardens, although they're rarely featured today. The current darling, *Impatiens walleriana* or busy Lizzie, was not commonly grown until the 1950s.

Matthiola
STOCKS

Grown in English gardens by the 16th century, stocks were available in double form by 1597. Valued for the tiny rose-like blossoms that line the stems, stocks are valuable as spring flowers, but go to seed and refuse to bud when the weather becomes hot. That quirk makes them perfect for British gardens, but not so well suited to most American flowerbeds. However, they remain a popular spring and fall crop and are flown in for use as cut flowers.

Mirabilis
FOUR O'CLOCK

As recently as the 1950s, four o'clocks were a fixture in the average flower garden, their bright yellow and magenta flow-

ers (often sporting both colors in the same flower or different colored flowers on the same stem) could be found everywhere. Nowadays, they're hard to find. Some surmise that it's the bright-colored blooms that sealed their fate. However, it could be that we no longer value flowers that only open for a few hours at the end of the day—although, at one time, their punctual late-afternoon performance was part of their charm. There is hope for a revival of interest.

Nicotiana
FLOWERING TOBACCO

At one time, fragrance was an important part of the appeal of

Nicotiana sylvestris

flowering tobacco, and it's hard to fathom why it was forfeited for a broader color range. With long, felted green leaves and loose stalks of majestic, trumpet-shaped blossoms, *Nicotiana* opens fully and sends its aroma pouring out after dark. That trait was perfect for early-20th-century ladies who wanted to preserve their peaches-and-cream complexions and yet enjoy a moonlit garden. Introduced in the late 19th century, flowering tobacco arrived just in time to coincide with the craze for moon gardens.

Papaver
POPPY

The opium or lettuce poppy, *Papaver somnifera*, was probably introduced into Britain by the Romans, and there were white, rose, violet, and striped versions quite early. Shirley poppies didn't appear until 1880, when the Vicar of Shirley set to work selecting a strain of *Papaver rhoeas* that sported a white hem around the edge of each blush-pink petal.

Petunia
PETUNIA

Fragrance was the most interesting trait that the first petunia to be classified could claim. The white *Petunia axillaris* (formerly *Petunia nyctaginiflora*), discovered in South America in 1823, had intensely night-scented, muddy white flowers. More interesting was the purple-blossomed *Petunia integritolia* (formerly *Petunia violacea*) found in Buenos Aires in 1831. By 1837, petunias were being interbred, resulting in fringed, bicolored, and semi-double flowers. Double forms followed shortly thereafter.

Phlox drummondii
DRUMMOND'S PHLOX

During the first half of the 20th century, no garden was complete without Drummond's phlox, introduced from Texas in the 1830s by Thomas Drummond. In the wild, its colors include rose, white, buff, pink, red, and purple. By the 1860s, the color range had expanded further, and by 1874 Drummond's phlox could boast the addition of varying-colored eyes accenting each blossom. How quickly we forget! Although this sun-loving annual has all the attributes of a superstar, it is a rarity in the garden. A revival could be in the offing.

Reseda
MIGNONETTE

Another casualty of fashion, mignonette was once an extremely important nosegay flower, especially when the streets were foul smelling and sweetly scented blooms were essential. One of the sweetest flowers grown, mignonette reputedly came to Europe from the Mediterranean before the 1st century. The unique orange and green blossoms have a strange form, resembling the setting for a diamond on a ring when the gem isn't yet installed. However, they dislike hot weather and quickly go out of bloom in the heat.

A variety of heirloom zinnias.

Tagetes
MARIGOLD

By the 16th century, marigolds had arrived in Europe, and they were popular garden plants. But there was little interest in a dwarf variety until the 1950s. Before that, the plants stood 18 inches or taller, with tansy-like, pungently scented leaves topped by daisy-like flowers in pale yellow.

Tropaeolum
NASTURTIUM

The nasturtium that we all know and love, *Tropaeolum majus*, came into cultivation in the 1600s and became an instant success. Festively colored red-, orange-, and yellow-flowered versions naturally occur in the wild, leaving little necessity for selective breeding.

Zinnia
ZINNIA

Hailed as the newest novelty on the current plant scene, *Zinnia peruviana* was actually the first member of the genus to arrive in Britain, in 1753. Holding small, mustard- or mulberry-colored flowers atop lanky three-foot stems, it didn't compare favorably with *Zinnia elegans,* which was introduced in 1796. It was *Zinnia elegans*, with its bright scarlet or crimson rayed, Mexican hat-shaped flowers, that became the parent of the many hybrids we know today. By 1856, there were double forms.

AN INTERVIEW WITH

RACHEL KANE

PERENNIALS OF
TIMES PAST

TOVAH MARTIN

I N A WAY, RACHEL KANE inherited her love of old-fashioned flowers. "Although my mother and grandparents were keen gardeners, I came to it largely through my father," she says. "He was a practicing landscape architect and he did the site plans for several National Trust properties." Many people are familiar with the work of Tom Kane. One of his best-known projects is Lyndhurst, a massive garden restoration along the Hudson River in Westchester County, New York.

With his interest in garden history, Tom Kane was definitely ahead of his time. "He was one of the few people involved with garden history during the 1960s and 70s, and he moved in a circle of people who shared his interest," Rachel recalls. It was through her father that she met Isadore Smith, who wrote about heirloom plants under the pen name of Ann Leighton. Rachel, who was in college at the time, says that their conversations were pivotal. "I remember that she was writing a series of books about American garden history, and she complained that there were no sources for the plants that she mentioned," Rachel recalls.

The scarcity of sources for old varieties was only part of the problem. At the time, perennials were not popular; annuals and foundation plantings reigned supreme. The fall of perennials had come with the Depression and World War II. "There simply wasn't sufficient labor to

Opposite: Hollyhocks at Rachel Kane's nursery. Heirloom flowers tend to be tall; dwarf varieties were uncommon until the 20th century.

keep up the vast perennial borders that were once popular in Britain," says Rachel. "Perhaps they survived in the small dooryard gardens of cottages, but people tended to exchange plants rather than purchase them. They didn't support the nurseries that governed supply and demand."

"When perennials lost their well-heeled clientele," she says, "styles essentially changed. The ball just stopped rolling." In addition, gardening in general declined as more people began to work away from home and spent less time on their properties. Perennials became difficult to find, and many of the very popular, older sorts all but disappeared from cultivation. "There was general difficulty getting anything but geraniums and wax begonias," Rachel remembers. "Even the common feverfew was very difficult to find." It became Rachel's self-inflicted task to find the old-fashioned beauties.

FERRETING OUT ANTIQUE PLANTS

In the 1980s, Rachel finished up her degree in plant and soil science. ("There wasn't a course in real horticulture back then, and they didn't teach us much about plants," she says.) She then started a nursery called Perennial Pleasures, based in East Hardwick, Vermont.

In her effort to ferret out antique plants, she combed through many catalogs. "Only a limited number of named plant varieties were available," she explains. "You had to look through a lot of catalogs and each offered perhaps only one plant that you were interested in collecting." To find the plants that she wanted, Rachel went as far afield as the Chelsea Physic Garden in London.

Finding heirlooms was a challenge, but growing them was also a difficult feat. "I made lists of plants that could grow in this climate," she says. Indeed, wintering perennials in upper Vermont, Zone 3, was not simple. "Thankfully, with our bountiful snow cover, we can grow perennials that are normally listed as hardy no farther north than Zone 5. Anything that will go underground in winter works here. Exotic woody plants that stick up above the snow cannot survive."

The plants she sought were markedly different from modern hybrids. "Things have changed drastically. Perennials have been made shorter and more manageable. During the 20th century, the emphasis has been on plants that are tidy," Rachel says. In fact, dwarf varieties were not common in the 19th century. "Delphiniums are a good case in point. The older delphiniums are closer to the original species than those we grow today." She advises anyone seeking out heirlooms to concentrate on taller plants: "Look for the taller

Unlike today's eight-inch-high varieties, antique sweet Williams are tall, and they are also fragrant.

varieties—they'll be the older types."

There is also more diversity among the individuals of heirloom varieties. When she grows these from seed, she finds greater variation in a row of seedlings. Nowadays, varieties are bred for uniformity. Rachel calls the hybrids that appeared from the 1950s onward "cookie-cutter plants."

Older varieties feature another important virtue. "They have greater vigor," she claims. "They're more resistant to the weather and diseases. They might not look as tidy, but they're stronger."

Fragrance was a critical factor to gardeners in earlier days, and it has diminished considerably with time. Rachel has sought to reintroduce fragrance into the garden. Not only has she made it her mission to collect fragrant phlox from old barnyards throughout Vermont and wherever she travels, but she also features named varieties of sweet Williams selected for their tall stems and sweet aroma. "People think of sweet Williams as eight inches tall now, but that's not what sweet Williams are all about."

Rachel noticed that heirloom perennials often produced smaller or fewer flowers per stem. "They weren't as floriferous, but they were more reliable and adaptable," she notes. "A good example would be the dreadful Pacific Giant primroses. They look so impressive with their huge flower umbels all faced upward in a pot when you purchase them in a supermarket. But they don't survive. You bring them home and they die," Rachel says. "Compare them to their parent species, *Primula vulgaris*. It has smaller flowers, but many more, and they're lovely—and they thrive. They don't just survive, they flourish."

DUBIOUS IMPROVEMENTS

Rachel has found that many so-called "advances" and "novelties" have weakened various perennials. Her favorite example is *Lobelia cardinalis* 'Queen Victoria', developed for its red leaves. "But it never sur-

A FEW OF RACHEL KANE'S FINDS

WHITE MARSH MARIGOLD, *Caltha palustris* var. *alba*—A white variant of the native yellow-flowered marsh marigold.

GOLDEN FEVERFEW, *Chrysanthemum parthenium* var. *aurea*—From the second half of the 19th century, "this golden version was used extensively in carpet bedding schemes," according to the Perennial Pleasures catalog.

CHOCOLATE FOXGLOVE, *Digitalis parviflora*—Rachel named this foxglove for its flowers that open reddish chocolate-brown.

LEMON LILY, *Hemerocallis lilio-asphodelus*—Smaller than newer daylilies, these are more delicate and especially loved for their strong lily-of-the-valley fragrance. The plant was called "custard lily" at the turn of the century, according to the Perennial Pleasures catalog.

THUNBERG'S DAYLILY, *Hemerocallis thunbergii*—First listed for sale in 1873, it features flowers that are lemon-yellow but with a green tinge to the outer petals.

THOMAS HOGG HOSTA, *Hosta decorata* 'Thomas Hogg'—This earliest-named cultivar of hosta in the U.S. has matte green leaves with a silver margin and dark lilac flowers.

vives here; it fails every year. The species has only plain green leaves, but it is a survivor." Modern sweet violets might hold their flowers higher above the foliage, but they've lost all their fragrance. "People don't know what they're missing compared to the old, true sweet violets," she says.

Individual perennials have gone in and out of fashion. "Asters were very big at the turn of the century in Britain, and to a lesser extent here, but they dropped from sight in the 1930s," she notes. The lemon lily, *Hemerocallis lilio-asphodelus,* is another example of a plant that has waltzed in and out of the public's affections. "Lemon lilies have a slender grace and a delicate fragrance that is utterly lacking in most modern varieties," she points out. "They also blend into a perennial border with greater ease because of their scale. These and other

WHITE ROSE CAMPION, *Lychnis coronaria* 'Oculata'—A 17th-century version with white flowers sporting a rose-pink center.

ROSE PLANTAIN, *Plantago major* 'Rosularis'—Cultivated since the 1500s, "This variety is most curious and rare, straight from the monastery and physic gardens. This species set foot on North American soil only one pace behind the earliest settlers," Rachel writes in her catalog.

HOSE-IN-HOSE PRIMROSE, *Primula* Pruhonicensis Hybrids—"It gives the appearance of one flower sprouting from within another; I offer a pale butter-yellow version," says Rachel.

White rose campion, *Lychnis coronaria* 'Oculata'.

Tall and willowy, heirloom perennials may not look as tidy as their modern counterparts, but many are more resistant to disease.

species daylilies have been trampled underfoot in the current frenzy of daylily hybridization."

On the subject of cup-and-saucer Canterbury bells, she becomes particularly incensed. "Modern cup-and-saucer Canterbury bells are extremely difficult to grow well," she points out. "So often, the 'saucer' looks as though it has had tea spilled on it, and it sags disgracefully around the 'cup'. The older, smaller-cupped varieties are far more satisfactory in the garden by comparison. Bigger is not necessarily better! Where is the charm in a six-inch-wide flower?"

Saponaria is still another heirloom perennial that has fallen victim to changing times and horticultural tastes. Rachel thinks she knows the reason. "Its common name is soapwort. And anything with a *wort* on the end is avoided nowadays. People have become so squeamish."

A COMPENDIUM OF OLD-FASHIONED PERENNIALS AND BIENNIALS

TOVAH MARTIN

Achillea
YARROW

Used as a medicinal herb since ancient times, *Achillea millefolium* forma *rosea*, the pink yarrow, appeared in Britain in the late 16th century and was immediately welcomed into the cottage garden. The golden yarrow, *Achillea filipendulina,* a later introduction, appeared by the second half of the 19th century. Yarrows have ferny foliage on tall stems topped by clusters of colorful blooms. They bloom toward midsummer, extending the perennial show.

Aconitum
MONKSHOOD

A favorite for cottage gardens and perennial borders alike, *Aconitum napellus,* alias monkshood, bears delphinium like spires of purplish blue blossoms on 2½-foot tall, fern-leaved stems. The name, monkshood, refers to the flower's

The pink yarrow, *Achillea millefolium.*

shape—the darkly colored blossoms resemble a monk's cowl. The plant was grown in monastery gar-

Left: columbine, *Aquilegia canadensis.* Right: wormwood, *Artemisia absinthium.*

dens and listed as indispensable for 13th-century physicians, despite its poisonous qualities.

Alcea
HOLLYHOCK
Introduced into Britain in 1573, hollyhocks were first employed medicinally to soothe swellings in horses' heels. A favorite in cottage gardens ever since, hollyhocks have broad, rounded, or fig-leaved foliage and spires of open-faced and wide-eyed blossoms that can rise, if well fertilized, six feet or more above the soil. The flowers come in yellow, shades of pink, and rose, often with a darker "eye" of a different shade. 'Nigra', a chocolate-burgundy version, was grown by Thomas Jefferson at Monticello. Thanks to the Thomas Jefferson Center for Historic Plants, it is enjoying another flirt with popularity at present.

Alchemilla
LADY'S MANTLE
Valued for its rounded, serrated leaves that hold dewdrops like jewels set in a necklace, and also for the cloud of yellow blossoms that rival baby's breath as a cut flower, Lady's mantle was introduced into the garden by the 14th century.

Aquilegia
COLUMBINE
Another favorite of British cottagers, columbines feature a unique flower that resembles a rocket shooting downward. The

British grew the short-spurred *Aquilegia vulgaris* for centuries before John Tradescant the Younger introduced the long-spurred *Aquilegia canadensis* into Britain. During the 1600s, gardeners cultivated striped columbines, which no longer exist.

Artemisia
WORMWOOD

Although not a blooming plant, artemisia's lacy silver foliage forms handsome accents in an heirloom garden. Wormwood, *Artemisia absinthium*, an extremely hardy and effective foliage plant, was once an essential medicinal herb used as an insect repellant and a cure for worms.

Dianthus
PINKS

Dianthus in all its many forms has played a seminal role in gardens for 2,000 years, at least. The most beloved is *Dianthus plumarius*, parent of so many 16th-century cinnamon pinks (also known as clove pinks), including 'Queen of Sheba' and 'Nonsuch', which are still available. Grown as garden flowers, cinnamon pinks feature blue-green, grass-like foliage with inch-wide blossoms in shades of white to pink, but the rich, spicy scent is the most enticing feature. Carnations, from *D. caryophyllus*, have longer stems and larger flowers, but less aroma. However, they're valued for their keeping quality: Carnations can last a week or more in bouquets. Sweet Williams, from *D. barbatus*, are

now nearly scentless. The older sweet Williams had long stems and rings of deep burgundy and pearly white on their blossoms.

Geranium
CRANESBILL

Called cranesbills by virtue of their long, "beaked" seedpods, geraniums have a bounty of small, colorful blossoms crowning a mound of deeply serrated leaves. Colors vary from lavender to maroon with a full complement of pinks and white to nearly black blooms. Three geraniums were already common in cultivation in the 16th century: *G. pratense*, *G. phaeum*, and *G. sanguineum*.

Hemerocallis
DAYLILY

Daylilies arrived in Britain in the 1570s with the French Huguenots. One of the earliest is the delightfully fragrant lemon lily, *H. lilioasphodelus* (formerly *H. flava*).

Iris
FLEUR-DE-LIS

The fact that many flowers were called lilies in the past has led to much confusion, especially with the common name of the iris, fleur-de-lis, or flower of the lily. Irises, in fact, are not related to lilies, although their blossoms are every bit as beautiful. The moisture-loving *Iris pseudacorus* has lined streams and rivers in Europe since earliest times, inspiring the French to take the flower as their emblem in the 6th century. Iris was named for the Greek goddess of the rain-

bow, and true to name, the droop-
ing flowers come in all colors, rising above sword-shaped leaves.

Lavandula
LAVENDER
Cultivated commercially as a perfume plant and grown in gardens
for the beauty of its gray-green
foliage topped by spikes of lilac-colored blossoms, lavender is a well-
known heirloom plant. The earliest
monastery gardens included lavender for its medicinal qualities.
Later, it was valued for its clean
scent; back in the 17th century,
lavender was associated with freshly washed linens.

**The earliest monastery gardens includ-
ed lavender for its medicinal qualities.**

Lilium
LILY
The oldest plant in cultivation is
thought to be the Madonna lily,
Lilium candidum, and that lily was
the only member of the family
known in Europe before the 16th
century. Subsequently, the
Madonna lily came to North
America, arriving at Plymouth in
the 1630s. Richly perfumed, the
waxen white trumpets are perched
on tall, brittle stems with shiny,
deep green leaves. Later, the
Turk's cap lilies *(L. martagon)* and
the regal lily *(L. regale)* became
popular.

Lupinus
LUPINE
Lupines didn't really make a major
splash on the horticultural scene
until 1937, when George Russell
introduced his group of hybrids,
which improved upon the species
dramatically. Suddenly, the plump
spires of pea-shaped flowers were
available in red, deep pink, orange,
and yellow, and bicolored blossoms appeared as well. And the
flower spikes had been rendered
taller and broader with many more
blossoms per spire rising above
palm-shaped leaves.

Lychnis coronaria
ROSE CAMPION
Lychnis coronaria, a handsome
accent in any garden, is also
known as mullein pink because of
its felted silver leaves, which form
a mullein-like rosette in the first
year before sending up blooming
spikes in the second. The original

Left: rose campion, *Lychnis coronaria*. Right: bee balm, *Monarda didyma*.

version had deep magenta flowers on top of tall stems. By the 17th century a white form was also available.

Macleaya
PLUME POPPY

Grown under the name bocconia, the plume poppy made its way into cultivation from China and Japan by 1866. Although it was suggested as a lawn accent, "as an isolated specimen," or as a potted plant, macleaya can't be contained for long. Fortunately, since they tend to pop up all over, plume poppies are handsome plants with large, oak-shaped, bluish green leaves on stems that stand eight feet or taller. By midsummer, they're crowned with yellow plumes like astilbe.

They spread by root stock as well as seed. Plume poppies are undeniably handsome, but they're bullies.

Monarda
BEE BALM

Monarda didyma, the bright-red-blossomed bee balm, was first introduced to Britain in 1744 by John Bartram, who discovered it near Lake Ontario. The scarlet whorls of flowers on this commonly used herb attract both bees and hummingbirds. The lightly mint-scented foliage is used for tea.

Myosotis
FORGET-ME-NOT

Forget-me-nots might have sentimental associations that make them seem like ancient flowers,

Forget-me-nots were introduced for garden use in the early 1800s.

but they weren't introduced until the early 1800s. Blooming in spring and prone to self-seeding, forget-me-nots form an ocean of tiny periwinkle-blue blossoms. The name was granted when a suitor reputedly knelt beside a raging river (where forget-me-nots are prone to grow) to pluck his sweetheart a fistful and was swept away, bellowing "forget me not" as he drowned.

Nepeta
CATNIP

Much to the delight of cats, *Nepeta cataria*—alias catnip—has been grown in gardens since 1265. The felted, grayish leaves emit a musky aroma that cats find alluring (to put it mildly). By 1672, catnip had already entered North America and escaped into the wild. More ornamental is *N. racemosa*, catmint, introduced to Britain in 1804. Catmint doesn't send felines into quite the same rapture, but it has clouds of purple, blossom-packed spires rising above the tiny, deeply textured, gray leaves.

Paeonia
PEONY

The first peony to enter Europe was *Paeonia mascula*, "the male peionie," used to cure men of epilepsy in the 6th century. Later came *P. officinalis*, employed to cure women of the same disease. Native to Siberia, Mongolia, and northern China, *P. lactiflora* reached British shores in 1784 and became the parent of the garden peonies we know today. Some of the oldest hybrids still in cultivation include 'Edulis Superba'

(1824), 'Festiva Maxima' (1851), and 'Duchesse de Nemours' (1856).

Phlox
SUMMER PHLOX
See page 71.

Primula
PRIMROSE
Primroses were considered important healing flowers from the Greeks onward. They were also beloved for their association with fairies, elves, and all the other mischief that goes on in the forest. Several primroses have figured prominently in history, including *Primula vulgaris*, the common, pale yellow primrose most often found in woodlands, with fragrant flowers held singly on a stem rising above a rosette of long, slender, pea-green leaves. The cowslip, *P. veris*, was more likely to be found in meadows and boasted a candelabra-like grouping of flowers held above its rosette of leaves. Most valued among the primrose varieties was the hose-in-hose form—a flower within a flower. The Jack-in-the-green version has a collar of green around each flower's neck, while the Jackanapes-on-horseback has a combination of leaves and petals.

Saponaria
BOUNCING BET
Although bouncing Bet becomes so rampant that it is often accused of being a weed, it was once an important part of cottage gardens. The reason for its prevalence was partly practical. In addition to

boasting softly colored pink and white flowers (now seen almost solely in double form), the plant was used as a substitute for soap, hence another common name—soapwort. When you rub it between your hands, the leaves produce a lather that has cleansing properties.

Tanacetum
FEVERFEW
Feverfew flings its seeds around so readily that it's scarcely valued in modern gardens. However, from the 17th century onward, feverfew was essential in herb and ornamental gardens. Part of its primary allure was its medicinal qualities. As the name implies, it reduces fever and,

Feverfew was essential in early herb and ornamental gardens.

more recently, it has also become valued as a cure for migraines. Feverfew has lacy leaves like those of artemisia, and is crowned by loose umbels of single, button-like, white daisy flowers with a prominent yellow center, like chamomile.

Valeriana
GARDEN HELIOTROPE

This workhorse of the perennial garden has sharply cut leaves on tall, three- to four-foot stems carrying umbels of white flowers that linger for several weeks in mid-summer. Although it might resemble heliotrope, the scent is not nearly as delightful. In fact, the plant might more accurately be described as pungent. The roots have been used medicinally since medieval times.

Viola
VIOLETS

It's little wonder that violets, native throughout the world, came early into gardens. They're modest plants; their rosettes of heart-shaped leaves creep shyly along the ground while demure blossoms are often hidden in the foliage. But due to the fragrance of the original *Viola odorata*, violets have figured strongly in poetry, prose, politics, and horticulture. Napoleon chose the fragrant violet as the emblem for the House of Bonaparte, provoking his supporters to wear the blossom in their buttonholes to show their support when he was exiled. Much later, in the United States, violets became an important nosegay flower, sold on city street corners and worn to the opera. As a result, violets were bred for larger flowers, longer stems, and disease resistance, to the detriment of the scent. Now it's difficult to find a truly fragrant violet. Scented heirloom varieties include the double Parma violets such as 'Lady Hume Campbell' (1875), 'Swanley White'(1880), 'Marie Louise' (1865), and 'Duchess de Parme' (1870).

Pansies, *V. × wittrockiana,* were developed in the 1820s and 1830s from the cross between *Viola tricolor, V. lutea,* and several other wild violet species. Named varieties were so popular by 1835 that 400 were available, and they became a favorite show plant by 1841.

Pansies were developed in the 1820s.

THE FABULOUS
PHLOX PANICULATA

RACHEL KANE

YOU KNOW THE SUMMER IS RIPE when the phlox are in bloom. Is it any wonder that these tall, strong-growing, floriferous, fragrant, late-blooming, long-lived, and many-colored plants have been the backbone of herbaceous perennial borders since the late 19th century?

There are approximately 60 recognized phlox species, including the moss pink (*Phlox subulata*), wild sweet William (*P. divaricata*), creeping phlox (*P. stolonifera*), and annual Drummond's phlox (*P. drummondii*). But when a gardener speaks of phlox, we all know exactly what he or she means—the comforting bodyguard of the summer garden, *Phlox paniculata*.

Common names include tall phlox, garden phlox, and summer phlox. The name phlox, like fish, seems to work as both singular and plural. In Greek, the genus name, *Phlox,* means flame, a good allusion to the often brightly colored flowers. However, since the only non-American species of phlox is native to Siberia, it's safe to assume that

Garden phlox has long been the backbone of perennial borders.

71

the Greeks never grew, encountered, or wove garlands of the flower. The species name, *paniculata,* simply alludes to the fact that the flowers are arranged in panicles.

The many varieties of *P. paniculata* that now exist have all sprung from the North American native, which originated along the Ohio River in Indiana, its range gradually spreading to Arkansas, northern Georgia, northeastern Kansas, and central New York. And wherever it sprang up, slightly different characteristics developed. Generally, the flower color in the wild is dull purple or magenta, but occasionally white or pink flowers will appear.

DOMESTICATING THE WILD PHLOX

First observed in 1700, *Phlox paniculata* was introduced into Britain in 1732 by Dr. James Sherard, where it quickly found a place in cottage gardens. Garden phlox grew happily in the cool, moist climate of Britain, but for some reason those early plants rarely produced seed there. This quirk made it necessary to propagate the plant primarily by root cuttings, which explains why few new varieties were developed by British gardeners.

In 1812, a Mr. Lyons of England imported a fresh batch of *P. paniculata* and named his imports *P. decussata,* under which name they were disseminated in the trade. He seems to have set an unfortunate trend, for during the early part of the 19th century, a number of European nurserymen imported *P. paniculata,* each giving a different name to their imports, much to the confusion of everyone. Some of the names include *P. cordata, P. corymbosa, P. scabra, P. sickmani, P. americana,* and *P. macrophylla*—all of which were actually nothing more exotic than *Phlox paniculata.*

Meanwhile, different hybrids certainly existed in the wild, showing some slight variations in leaf or flower. But they were (and are) all technically *P. paniculata.* Traces of this grab bag of names persist in garden books and catalogs today, causing great anguish for more than a few garden restorationists searching for particular varieties.

The first English hybrid was introduced in 1824 by G. Wheeler, a nurseryman in Warminster who gave his novelty the humble name of *P.* 'Wheelerii'. Apparently, he set a paternal precedent, for it was followed by *P.* 'Shepardii', introduced by S. Shepard of Bedford, and *P.* 'Coldryana', raised by Mr. Coldry of Bristol, among others. But real progress on the species began in France, starting in 1839 with the work of a hybridizer by the name of M. Lierval, whose efforts produced larger and more rounded

Opposite: *Phlox paniculata* 'Bright Eyes' is a classic cultivar that dates back to 1934. It is growing here with tansy.

corollas, many new colors, and larger and longer flower panicles. Cultivars appeared rapidly from that date onward.

A FONDNESS FOR PHLOX

Phlox have won our esteem on many accounts. The majority of cultivars bloom courageously in the torpid months of July and August and have enough substance to "carry" the perennial border through the hot months until the fall asters, anemones, and monkshood can pick up the baton. With the variety of shades available you can have a garden full of fresh color long after the early summer favorites such as irises, peonies, and bellflowers have faded. Each plant of *P. paniculata* generally blooms for

THE BEST CLASSIC CULTIVARS

'AMETHYST'—Mentioned by 1949, it has reddish pink flowers by day, changing to a violet-blue in the evening or on cloudy days.

'BLUE BOY'—Mentioned by 1945, it has pale blue-violet flowers.

'BRIDESMAID'—Mentioned by 1910, it has white flowers suffused with palest pink and a rose-pink eye.

'BRIGADIER'—Mentioned by 1959, its flowers are soft red with touches of orange and deep pink.

'BRIGHT EYES'—Dating to 1934, it was originally known as 'Daily Sketch'. It has clear shell pink flowers accented by a deep pink eye.

'CHARLES CURTIS'—Dating to 1940, it has soft sunset red blossoms.

'ELIZABETH CAMPBELL'—Mentioned by 1930, it has flowers with salmon shading and a pink tinge.

'GRAF ZEPPELIN'—Mentioned by 1934, the flowers are pure white with a clearly defined carmine eye.

'LEO P. SCHLAGETER'—Introduced in 1934. Its long-blooming flowers are strong, bright pink.

'RIJNSTROOM'—Introduced in 1910, this favorite of Louise Beebe Wilder has small florets and rich, salmon-pink flowers.

nearly a month, but by combining early and late bloomers, you can enjoy bloom from late June through late September.

Phlox paniculata comes in a wide variety of colors. Stark to pearly white, orchid pink to hot pink, pale lilac to soft purple, salmon to just a breath away from true orange, red-violet to cherry red, and, of course, the original magenta—a color much maligned by present-day garden columnists. The flowers may be a solid color, or they may have a paler or deeper eye. Some even change color according to the weather or the time of day.

Many phlox, particularly the old-fashioned varieties, have a light, fresh fragrance tinged with a touch of spice. It is the summer scent of your grandmother's garden. It is nothing so romantic as jasmine, or as exuberant as roses, or as sharp as clove pinks. In fact, the aroma of garden phlox

---

'SIR JOHN FALSTAFF'—Mentioned by 1958. Its florets are large and salmon-pink.

'TRAPIS BLANC'—Introduced in 1901 and also known as 'Mia Ruys', it is short in height with pure white flowers.

'WIDAR'—Introduced in 1912. Its flowers have bright reddish violet florets with large white centers.

Phlox paniculata 'Widar'.

An heirloom mix of garden phlox. Most cultivars bloom courageously through the torpid months of July and August, and many of the older varieties show natural resistance to powdery mildew.

is so soft and pervasive that it has become synonymous with the smell of a luscious midsummer night.

KEEPING PHLOX HEALTHY

Phlox are fast-growing perennials, and with proper feeding, the paltriest shoot will reach a decent size within three years. They are large, strong plants that will create a solid presence in the border, and are upright enough to create four-foot "walls" dividing up space without the use of "hard structure." Healthy plants never need staking.

In the wild, phlox are found in mineral-rich soils, especially in limey regions and along streams. This gives a gardener a clue about how to treat them in the garden. They grow best if given plenty of water during the summer; the quality of the plants will suffer noticeably if they are kept dry. Depending on where you live a very important soil amendment is limestone to keep the soil from becoming acid. The proper pH goes a long way to keeping phlox healthy and powdery-mildew free.

Although they are very long-lived plants and can often be found thriving in long abandoned gardens, garden phlox are heavy feeders, and in order to maintain the quality of the flower trusses and the overall health of the plants, they should be lifted, divided, and planted in freshly enriched soil every three to five years.

Phlox fulfill their potential if grown in full sun, although partial shade, particularly in warmer regions of the country, is acceptable. A bit of shade also helps phlox with blue flowers maintain their color without fading.

The best time to plant bare-root garden phlox is in spring or fall. However, potted garden phlox can be planted throughout the summer. The added attraction of summer planting is that you can actually see the bloom color, rather than relying on inferior (and often faded) photo tags or woefully inadequate color descriptions. There is also a real problem with incorrectly identified plants, particularly in mass plant outlets, big retailers, and garden centers. So it does help to see what you're getting.

Garden phlox are troubled by few pest and disease problems. Powdery mildew is the most common complaint. Some varieties are particularly susceptible to the problem and will succumb no matter what you do. However, many of the old varieties show natural resistance to mildew. We find that mildew virtually disappears as long as the plants are divided regularly, the clumps thinned out to improve air circulation, and replanted into enriched sweet soil. Other preventive measures include watering adequately (in the morning rather than the evening) and avoiding overhead watering. In southern regions, powdery mildew is a particularly troublesome problem. Select resistant varieties—ask your local nursery, neighboring gardeners, or mail-order specialists for suggestions. Another simple solution is to plant other perennials in front to camouflage the unsightly foliage. Powdery mildew will not effect the longevity of your phlox.

In hot, dry weather, you might see the effects of red spider mites, which cause the leaves to yellow, curl, and eventually drop off. While unsightly, this damage is rarely life-threatening. The best preventive measure is to maintain the beds in fertile condition and water adequately.

RESTORING OLD VARIETIES

In the 1940s, over 200 named varieties of phlox were available in the United States. Many of these have been lost over the years as garden fashions have changed. The biggest losses occurred from the 1950s to the 1980s when perennial borders nearly ceased to exist, supplanted by the foundation planting craze and the infamous no-maintenance garden period. Thankfully, there has been an overall resurgence of interest, and phlox, as well as many other older plant varieties, have been rediscovered in old farmyards. They began to be sought out again in the small, out-of-the-way nurseries whose proprietors saw no reason to stop growing the good old plants. Some old varieties are still being grown in Europe and have been re-imported back to their homeland.

AN INTERVIEW WITH
ELLEN McCLELLAND LESSER

PERIOD FLOWER ARRANGEMENTS

TOVAH MARTIN

ELLEN McCLELLAND LESSER traces her interest in flower arranging back to her childhood. "Ever since I was a wee sprout I had a bouquet of flowers in my hands," she recalls. She grew up in northern Westchester County, New York, "which was very rural at the time." And she remembers the gardens of her youth. "They were overgrown 1920s gardens, so we had lilacs and phlox and wonderful scenes of something growing en masse around every bend. One of my great joys was going out with the dogs and picking flowers." Later, she went out with her mother, who taught her the names of the flowers. "And that's how summer evenings were spent," Ellen says.

"We always had flowers on the dining room table and I arranged them. My mother was incredibly patient about all the spiders that would fall off in the house. It surprised no one when I chose horticulture as an avenue of study in college," Ellen says. She took courses in landscape architecture, but she really hankered to learn floral history. Finding that there was no appropriate major in that topic, she composed her own custom curriculum of history and design.

Eventually, Ellen did an internship at the National Trust property of Chesterwood in Stockbridge, Massachusetts. Her interaction with that historic Daniel Chester French garden graphically demonstrated how blossoms have changed. "When I first came to Chesterwood, butterfly snapdragons were all the rage, and they weren't anything like the snapdragons I saw illustrated in period books. I also discovered that not all delphiniums are created equal, and I realized that marigolds were taller and single flowered back in the beginning of the century. So I launched a research project on the topic," Ellen recalls. Her studies led the historian to look further, but she found few references. Old paintings pro-

vided the most accurate and readily available color records of what was grown. The subjects for those old paintings were often still lives of bouquets. Suddenly, Ellen found all of her passions converging.

Her studies of that "obscure field" finally bore fruit 15 years ago at a meeting of the Victorian Society,

Bouquets of the Victorian era were colorful. Even those described as "tasteful and chaste" often included ten different flowers.

where Ellen met Jim Ryan of Olana, the home of the artist, Frederic Church, near Hudson, New York. "Jim asked me to do Christmas arrangements for Olana, and I envisioned a little holly here and there and that sort of thing," Ellen remembers. "But then he showed me pictures of the kind of arrangements he had in mind. They were more like architecture than arrangements." Ellen rose to the occasion. "I gave myself the short course in Victorian flower arranging, using Annie Hassard's book, *Floral Decorations for the Dwelling House,* published by Macmillan and Co. in 1876. I spent a lot of time at The New York Botanical Garden reading everything that I could find." As a result, she created a floral masterpiece perfectly true to period, and she's been creating similar extravaganzas at Olana ever since. The assignment has led to years of study in the field.

In the 19th and early 20th century, passion flower—or whatever flower happened to be in season—was used in arrangements.

FOREIGN INFLUENCES

In the course of her research, Ellen discovered that flower arrangements have changed drastically over the years: "The Japanese influence has been really profound. The Ikebana arrangement and its proportions have permeated our way of thinking. We use flowers in odd numbers like threes, we think in terms of height to dwarf the vase. But before the 1850s, when Admiral Perry sailed into Tokyo Harbor and opened Japan to the West, we did not think about arrangements that way. At first, the West was interested in their porcelains and textiles. But eventually we imported their florist work as well."

Before the 1850s, the proportions of bouquets were different and the components varied. These bouquets tended to boast a diversity of flowers and forms, and a bounty of colors. Foliage (or "filler," as it is now called) was a much more important element of the bouquet. "People used leaves, berries, and branches in their arrangements. Begonia leaves and croton and canna foliage were used, with yellow or red flowers interspersed to pick up the accent colors in the leaves,"

Ellen notes, "whereas modern arrangements often have no scrap of foliage." This may be due to changes in fashion, but from a purely practical point of view, modern cut flowers are often shipped long distances and arrive with damaged foliage, which is removed. Ellen has found that the chore became automatic. "It's become common practice to strip the foliage from the stems of roses and chrysanthemums, for example, even if the leaves have not been damaged."

There was good reason to employ additional foliage at a time before floral foam ("a post-1960s thing," says Ellen) arrived on the scene. The foliage provided a structural base for the flowers. "Originally, they had only frogs and wire hairpin holders. The pinholder as we know it came from the Far East." And so the strategically placed greenery formed a grid to stabilize the flower stems. If the arranger needed more base, he or she used damp sand or sawdust or moss to hold an arrangement stable.

Arrangements were denser and larger than many of the pared down modern bouquets. Ellen has discovered that they were also more colorful. "The further you go back in time, the more colorful and mixed an arrangement might be. You read descriptions of bouquets that are referred to as 'tasteful and chaste' with ten different flowers stuffed in. The handheld bouquet was extremely complicated in color patterns. But in Edwardian England, many arrangements had only one kind of flower in one color—sweet peas, carnations, or autumn asters. The carnation was considered to be terribly chic. They were so aristocratic that you just did not mix them with other flowers, or even other shades of carnations. Unfortunately, now they're so common that they've become the dog food of cut flowers."

SEASONAL BOUQUETS

It's fascinating to trace the evolution of bouquets. Fashion has affected what is used in arrangements, but technology has had the strongest influence on dinner-table decorations. Before flowers could be flown in from warmer climates and the tropics, flower arrangers used whatever was on hand. Arrangements reflected the season. "Lily-of-the-valley was a common cut flower throughout the year," Ellen points out. "It was grown under glass (like violets) in local greenhouses and sold in the area or shipped short distances via rail. However, lily-of-the-valley does not ship well over long distances, so it is now available only in spring."

At one time, forget-me-nots played a major role as cut flowers. "You'd have forget-me-nots and roses combined in a luncheon arrangement," Ellen has found. Today's most common filler, baby's breath, was not available. "You don't even see it mentioned in perennial gardens until the 1880s and 1890s," she notes.

The repertoire of commonly used flowers has evolved. In the 19th and early 20th century, China asters, dahlias, violets, stevia, fuchsias, camellias, primroses, passion flower, bouvardia, verbenas, mignonette, orchids, and water lilies (!) were often used, although they aren't quite as popular today. Chrysanthemums were solely an autumn flower, and they were considered a luxury item—grown in greenhouses, where they were encouraged to produce one large flower on the tip of each stem. "A bouquet would only have one or two chrysanthemums because they were so precious," says Ellen. Other commonly used Victorian autumn flowers included Michaelmas daisies, China asters, heleniums, sneezeweed, goldenrods, tansy, and nasturtiums with accents of hops, maple, begonias, caladiums, coleus, geranium leaves, Japanese lanterns, and ferns. "The predominant colors for autumn were not oranges and yellows. They preferred jewel tones in their bouquets to accent that time of year."

Then there was the matter of shelf life—a factor that has limited our inventory of appropriate cut flowers. In the past, flowers weren't expected to last for a week or more. "They were the gift of an evening," says Ellen. "The ephemeral nature of flowers was part of their attraction." Initially, Ellen was amazed to find that maidenhair ferns, which perish rapidly, were used with such abandon. However, she had to keep in mind that they needed to be prime for only a few hours.

TABLETOP DRAMA

All of this knowledge comes into play when Ellen composes the annual Christmas arrangements at Olana. "At your typical Victorian dinner party, the dining room door was closed until dinner was served. So the table was set for the element of drama. The guests were expected to gasp in amazement when the doors were thrown open and they first beheld the table and its accoutrements," Ellen explains. And tables were scaled up accordingly. The table at Olana is nearly 58 inches wide and easily seats 12. The tablecloth was traditionally white, and the dinner was served individually to each guest by the wait-staff. Apparently, the serving method made a major difference in the scale of the table decorations. At one time each course was laid out in serving dishes and then parceled onto individual plates; at the conclusion

Opposite: Tabletop arrangements were often tall, including fruits as well as flowers.

Flowers commonly used in period arrangements include, clockwise from top left: annual asters, violets, and forget-me-not.

of each course the tablecloth was removed, as it had undoubtedly become stained as the food was shuffled around. "A meal was referred to as having two or three removes rather than courses," says Ellen. All the dishes in the table's center left ample room for arrangements, and you wouldn't want to fiddle with a too elaborate floral arrangement when removing a tablecloth to reveal the next course's linen underneath.

Not so with the Frederic Church household. They served dinner on individual plates and often featured a three-tiered epergne at the center of the table. "When filled with flowers, it stands a yard tall. Dining rooms traditionally had high ceilings and the table was so wide that you couldn't expect to speak with the person across from you," Ellen explains. As for the flowers, they were apt to include cyclamen, geraniums, calla lilies, cut poinsettias, cinerarias, and azalea branches as well as orchids. Beyond blossoms, the epergne often featured fruit such as grapes and pears dangling over its tiers.

Ellen makes two subsidiary arrangements to adorn the center of the table, and there are individual flowers at each place setting echoing the main theme—a rose, perhaps, with a piece of fern, galax or geranium leaf tucked into a fluted bud vase. There might be scented-leaved geranium leaves floating in the fingerbowls and around the fairy lamps (similar to votive lights). The Churches had no chandelier in their dining room, so light was furnished from candelabras, also placed on the table.

Ellen explains that it was common to place flowers, as if strewn, directly on the tablecloth, using tricolor geranium leaves set in a pattern. She also weaves garlands to be swagged over the doorways of the room. Olana is fitted with hooks set in the wall specifically for the purpose.

Her spread varies each year, but she keeps essential ingredients in mind. "Scented flowers were important. The smell of food was considered vulgar, and you wanted to mask it with fragrant flowers," Ellen discovered in her studies.

The art of flower arrangements was surprisingly different in the past. Before the 20th century, arrangers highlighted scent, featured the blossoms in seasons, and used vivid colors. The most important difference is that back then, floral arrangers relied solely on whatever happened to be in season. So if you decide to try your hand at period flower arranging, Ellen advises, "Never mix forsythia and peonies, or you're giving yourself away."

THE HISTORY OF
HOUSEPLANTS

TOVAH MARTIN

FOR MANY YEARS, I lived in a rambling Victorian house. It had all the elements that we associate with the 19th century—the bay windows, the drafty front parlor, the cavernous rooms, and the fringed furniture. It also had houseplants.

The houseplants fit perfectly with the prevailing milieu; they seemed comfortable in the house. And no wonder. Not only did the builder have houseplants in mind when he included bay windows in both front and back parlors, but everyone who had ever lived in the house from the 1890s onward grew plants in the windows. We had the photographs to prove it.

The fact is, the 19th century was a heyday for houseplants. Before the Industrial Revolution, a few ardent gardeners entertained plants indoors, but they were definitely in the minority. The average person didn't begin growing plants indoors until glass became less expensive and windows therefore grew larger. Houseplants weren't commonplace until furnaces were improved to allow more even distribution of heat. And the roster of available houseplants didn't swell until the Age of Exploration. Then, with more expedient modes of travel at their beck and call, botanists hastened tropicals back and forth, right into the eagerly awaiting hands of indoor gardeners.

IN THE BEGINNING, THERE WERE BULBS

Tropicals weren't a household word until mail-order nurseries began shipping plants and seeds. And it's amazing how rapidly American

nurseries managed to receive the newly introduced exotics, build their stock, propagate them, and offer the new rarities to the public. At first they offered seed, and exotics were incorporated into the seed lists of all the

Houseplants weren't common until glass became affordable and thus windows grew larger.

major seed houses. However, by the end of the 19th century, live plants were also being shipped throughout the eastern part of the United States.

When all those crucial components fell into place, the houseplant business burgeoned. Once houseplants became available, they were welcomed into the home with open arms. Of course, it was a gradual progression; indoor gardeners first tested the waters. It all began in the 1830s with bulbs such as hyacinths, tulips, paperwhites, daffodils, and crocus.

Spring bulbs were perfect for growing indoors. Not only could they endure the dark recesses of the average mid-century Victorian parlor, but they also tolerated the chilly temperatures typical of a time when homes weren't heated at night. In fact, hardy bulbs loved the cool temperatures in 19th-century homes: The flowers lingered longer when the temperature plummeted every night, and the bulbs performed just as well (if not better) than they did outdoors. The Victorians couldn't

Victorian parlors were chilly, especially at night—the perfect environment for perennials such as primroses. They were dug up from outdoors, given a good cutting-back, and brought indoors for the winter.

have found more auspicious plants with which to begin.

Bulb forcing was embraced with such fervor that special forcing vases were invented for the purpose. The most popular were hyacinth jars, but scaled-down crocus vases were also on the market. Gardeners filled urns with pocket-sized gardens of bulbs and made complex arrangements of forced bulbs as table centerpieces. Bulb-forcing became such a prevalent wintertime pursuit that it trickled down to every strata of society: Forced bulbs resided in mansions as well as modest cottages. They were omnipresent.

PERENNIALS IN THE PARLOR

Victorian gardeners now had the confidence to move forward. The parlor was still frosty overnight, especially in the recesses of the windowsills, so perennials were an obvious next step. Perennials demanded cool temperatures overnight, and that's just what the parlor could furnish. Many gardeners dug roses, violets, and primroses from their flower beds in autumn, gave them a severe cutting-back (especially roses and other perennials with wandering branches), and brought them indoors for the winter, where they sprouted anew and bore blossoms. By this time, glass was cheaper and more readily available, so windows were larger and the average home was bright enough to support blossoming perennials.

Again, this was something that everyone could embrace, regardless of their economic situation. As long as gardeners had a few extra minutes to fetch water in a watering pot, as long as they managed to find some spare time to dig a plant or two in autumn, and had a modest windowsill large enough to support a pot, they could enjoy the benefits of plants indoors. Magazines went so far as to give directions for pinning acorns to the wallpaper, where they would sprout in the heat. They even offered instructions on dropping grass seed into the crevices of pine cones and watching the seed sprout as the cones

FLOWERING TROPICALS PREVALENT IN LATE 19TH-CENTURY WINDOWSILLS

Abutilon	Jasminum
Allamanda	Mandevilla
Azalea	(known then
Begonia	as Dipladenia)
Bouvardia	Mimulus
Browallia	Nerium
Brugmansia	Oxalis
Camellia	Passiflora
Cereus	Pelargonium
Cestrum	Pentas
Chrysanthemum	Piqueria
Citrus	Pittosporum
Clerodendrum	Plumbago
Daphne	Russellia
Datura	Salvia
Gardenia	Skimmia
Heliotropium	Sparmannia
Hibiscus	Stephanotis
Hoya	Tropaeolum
Impatiens	Verbena

began to swell open in the heat from a furnace. Everyone, no matter his or her station in life, could enjoy the beauty of houseplants.

Houseplants provided spiritual inspiration as well. Nature was seen as an inherently good influence; Victorians believed that by bringing nature indoors, the moral fiber of family members would be strengthened. When the population began moving to the cities, away from the familiar rural foundations of family life, houseplants went along, lest the simple goodness of nature would be forgotten.

BRINGING THE TROPICS INDOORS

Ferns and other foliage plants were the first tropical plants to be cultivated indoors. They didn't require the high light levels that bloomers demanded. And they could also endure fluctuating temperatures. Always eager to make the best of the situation at hand, Victorian gardeners assured each other that foliage plants were superior to their blossoming counterparts; only unsophisticated gardeners, they deigned, required the gratification of blossoms.

By the end of the 19th century, blossoming tropicals became the rage, and the selection quickly expanded. Before long, passion flowers, citrus, camellias, abutilons, geraniums, daturas, daphnes, pentas, and impatiens—to name only a handful of the plants that became readily available—all became household words. Magazines proliferated to explain exactly how gardeners might host their photosynthesizing houseguests. Gardeners pruned their plants with care to encourage maximum growth and bud production, and bathed them more frequently than most family members bathed. They cracked windows open to provide their exotics with fresh air, and took them outdoors to spray them with nicotine when insects threatened. At regular intervals, they applied manure tea in generous doses. If frost threatened the parlor (which it occasionally did, despite the prevalence of central heating), they covered the entire menagerie with blankets. And they displayed their plants with pride in the gathering places of the house. The windowsill garden was furnished with all the bells and whistles: statues, fountains, aquariums, and perhaps a birdcage or two with the obligatory canary.

And that's exactly what the photographs of the Victorian parlor where I used to live depict. They show Grandpa Logee reclining in his overstuffed easy chair beside a bay window filled to brimming with begonias, parlor palms, and citrus. Everything is lush, the plants are in good health, and Grandpa Logee is looking duly proud. His favorite watering can is not far away.

A COLLECTION OF HEIRLOOM HOUSEPLANTS

TOVAH MARTIN

Allamanda cathartica
GOLDEN TRUMPET

A Brazilian native introduced in 1846, this robust vine was a favorite in bay windows, where it received the abundant light so essential to its well-being. No fewer than five varieties of the most popular species, *Allamanda cathartica*, were in cultivation, the most popular being *Allamanda cathartica* 'Williamsii', with its huge, three- to four-inch, gaping, canary yellow, trumpet-shaped flowers. It is lightly scented of wine in the evening.

Begonia
BEGONIA

The Victorians were ardent begonia enthusiasts, their favorite group being the rex-cultorum, which was hybridized so that nearly every color of the rainbow was represented in the ornamental foliage. Also prevalent in period catalogs were the angel-wing types and rhizomatous begonias. *Begonia × erythrophylla*, the beef-

Golden trumpet.

steak begonia, a rhizomatous type, was found on nearly every farmhouse windowsill. It remains a popular heirloom, coveted partly for its longevity.

91

Browallia
BROWALLIA
First introduced from South
America in 1798, browallias are
now grown primarily as annuals in
the outdoor garden. But during
Victorian times, their bright sky-
blue, star-shaped flowers were a
welcome addition to the sunny
windowsill.

Brugmansia
ANGEL'S TRUMPET
Together with the closely related
daturas, brugmansias satisfied the
Victorian penchant for hefty-sized
plants. Mature angel's trumpets
easily reach 10 to 12 feet, and the
bushes were often allowed to attain
their full stature outdoors during
their summer sojourn. In the fall,
they were severely pruned and
brought indoors for parlor decora-
tion. Most popular in the 19th century was *Brugmansia suaveolens*,
with its large, dangling, ghostly
white blossoms.

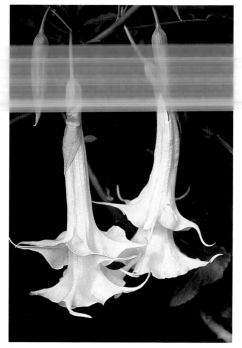

Angel's trumpet

Calceolaria
POCKETBOOK PLANT
Known as the slipperwort or pock-
etbook plant, calceolaria was a vast-
ly different and relatively unim-
pressive plant before it was
enhanced by European breeders
toward the end of the 19th century.
In North America, most Victorian
gardeners had access only to the
canary-yellow species with its small
but profuse pouch-like flowers. The

fact that the plants last only a single season bothered no one.

Clerodendrum thomsoniae
GLORY BOWER
Clerodendrum thomsoniae (known
in the 19th century as *C. balfouri*)
was the most popular member of
the genus in 1881, as it is today.
It's no wonder that the plant
achieved such all-encompassing
fame. Its large, balloon-like, white
bracts and red flowers are reminiscent of the bleeding hearts of the
garden, but the display continues
throughout most of the year if
afforded bright light.

Opposite: Angel wing begonias as well as the rex-cultorum group and the rhizomatous types were extremely popular Victorian houseplants.

Mandevilla, *M. x amabilis* 'Alice DuPont'. The Victorians grew white-flowered mandevillas as well as pinks.

Hibiscus rosa-sinensis
HIBISCUS
The double pink *Hibiscus rosa-sinensis* was highly valued for its huge, profuse blooms. Hibiscus boast all the traits that the Victorians valued, including brightly colored flowers, ample size, and ease of cultivation.

Mandevilla
MANDEVILLA
The fragrant *Mandevilla laxa* (once known as *M. suaveolens*) was introduced in 1837 and was frequently grown for its luminous, white, trumpet-shaped flowers. The pink-flowering *M. amabilis* (known then as *Dipladenia amoena*), which is now very popular as a houseplant, was occasionally grown in Victorian times, but its cultivation was primarily confined to greenhouses. At present, *M. x amabilis* 'Alice DuPont' is deservingly popular for its four-inch-wide, glowing pink trumpets, which brighten windowsills both summer and winter.

Mimulus
MONKEY FLOWER
With its yellow blossoms with red spots on the throat and reddish blotches on the lobes, *Mimulus luteus* was a frequent resident on sunny windowsills. Vying with *M. luteus* for fame was the musk plant, *M. moschatus*, a yellow-flowering, tender, North American native.

Nepenthes
PITCHER PLANTS
The Victorians were always enthu-

A variety of heirloom houseplants brighten a windowsill, including allamanda, clerodendrum, bougainvillea, and pentas.

siastic about any freak of nature, and pitcher plants certainly furnished bizarre subjects on which to lavish affection. Those weird and difficult-to-cultivate insectivores were grown for their strangely shaped insect-catching pitchers, which dangled ominously over the sides of hanging baskets. The first nepenthes was introduced in 1820. By the 1870s, several family members had reached North American shores.

Nerium
OLEANDER

Despite its poisonous properties, oleander was an indoor favorite. Double and single varieties were in cultivation, although the color range was limited to pink or white. Interestingly, according to Peter

Henderson, "a striped variety, with marks exactly like those of a carnation" was available, but it is no longer in the trade. Half the beauty of the older oleanders was the fragrance—reminiscent of macaroons. Newer hybrids are bred for brightly colored flowers and dwarf stature, to the detriment of the scent.

Olea
OLIVE

Although it rarely, if ever, blossoms indoors and isn't a particularly handsome plant, *Olea europaea* was grown indoors for its Biblical associations. Much more rewarding was *Osmanthus fragrans,* known to 19th-century gardeners as *Olea fragrans*, the sweet olive. Its tiny flowers emit the fragrance of stewed apricots.

Pentas lanceolata
EGYPTIAN STARS
Introduced from South Africa in 1842, this was a very deserving windowsill celebrity, now enjoying a comeback. *Pentas lanceolata* (grown in the 19th century as *Pentas carnea*) has profuse, star-shaped flowers in dense umbels throughout the year. The Victorians knew only the "flesh-colored" species, but we now have pink, red, white, and lavender hybrids, including dwarf forms.

Piqueria
STEVIA
Destined to become an important cut flower for the florist trade, stevia was grown as a filler for bouquets, performing the duties now relegated to baby's breath. Not only are the sprays of tiny flowers profuse and long-lasting, but they also have a sweet anise aroma. There is currently a grassroots effort to revive stevia for the cut-flower market.

Pittosporum tobira
MOCK ORANGE
First introduced in 1789, *Pittosporum tobira* has rhododendron-like, forest green leaves topped by umbels of intensely fragrant, cream-colored flowers. It remains a very popular indoor plant.

Plumbago
LEADWORT
The Victorians grew white, powder blue, and red varieties of plumbago. It was especially valuable clipped into standard (or tree) form. The flower umbels were also used as florist blossoms in the early 20th century.

Skimmia japonica
SKIMMIA
We grow this evergreen as a garden shrub south of Zone 6, but the Victorians often invited *Skimmia japonica* indoors along with another fragrant shrub, *Daphne odora*. Introduced in 1845, this native of Japan owed its popularity partly to its Oriental connection, but also to the fact that it could survive cool growing conditions.

Sparmannia africana
INDOOR LINDEN
This large and robust tropical rapidly becomes too sizable for the average home, but that didn't dampen the Victorian enthusiasm for the plant. Introduced from the Cape of Good Hope in 1790, *Sparmannia africana* traditionally was grown indoors in Europe, especially in Germany. The custom eventually crossed the ocean to North America.

Tropaeolum
NASTURTIUM
Nasturtiums were among the most popular hanging plants. Despite their tendency to attract insects, nasturtiums were especially popular after hybridizing began in the 1830s. The enhanced nasturtiums added shades of orange to the yellow species, as well as mottled petals.

NURSERY SOURCES

The following list of suppliers was compiled with information from the Flower and Herb Exchange.

AGUA FRIA
Route 6, Box 11A
Santa Fe, NM 87501
Tel: (505) 438-8888
www.plantsofthesouthwest.com
Southwestern native wildflowers, grasses, shrubs and trees, and heritage vegetables. $3.50 catalog.

AMERICAN DAYLILY & PERENNIALS
P.O. Box 210
Grain Valley, MO 64029
Tel: (816) 224-2852
400 varieties of Hemerocallis, some heirlooms.

ANTIQUE ROSE EMPORIUM
9300 Lueckemeyer Road
Brenham, TX 77833
Tel: (800) 441-0002
250 old landscape and garden roses.

B & D LILIES
P.O. Box 2007
Port Townsend, WA 98368
Tel: (360) 765-4341
Over 200 lilies, some rare and pre-1940.

BLUESTEM PRAIRIE NURSERY
13197 E. 13th Road
Hillsboro, IL 62049
Tel: (217) 532-6344
Plants native to Midwestern prairies and savannas. Seeds are sold by packet, and by custom mixes from November through February. Plants are sold bare root in March and April; plant orders should be in by mid-February. Free catalog.

W. ATLEE BURPEE & CO.
Warminster, PA 18974
Tel: (800) 888-1447
Heirloom vegetables, herbs, and flowers.

CANYON CREEK NURSERY
3527 Dry Creek Road
Oroville, CA 95965
Tel: (530) 533-2166
Heirloom flowering plants.

COMPANION PLANTS
7247 N. Coolville Ridge Road
Athens, OH 45701
Tel: (740) 592-4643
More than 600 varieties of common and exotic herbs, many turn-of-the-century and settler varieties.

THE COOK'S GARDEN
P.O. Box 5010
Hodges, SC 29653
Tel: (800) 457-9703
http://st6.yahoo.com/cooksgarden/index.html
"Seeds and Supplies for the New American Kitchen Garden" includes a nice selection of heirloom herbs and flowers. All seeds are untreated.

COOLEY'S GARDENS
P.O. Box 126-BB
Silverton, OR 97381
Tel: (503) 873-5463
400 varieties of tall bearded iris. $5 catalog.

DABNEY HERBS
Box 22061
Louisville, KY 40252
Tel: (502) 893-5198
Specializes in herbs with some pre-1800 heirlooms. Organically grown and nursery-propagated plants.

DEEP DIVERSITY SEED
P.O. Box M
Corvallis, OR 97339
Tel: (505) 438-8080
A botanical seed collection of rare and obscure ornamentals, flowers, herbs, and vegetables. Unique catalog lists plants by taxonomic group ($4, refunded on orders of $20 or more).

DEGIORGI SEED COMPANY
6011 N. Street
Omaha, NE 68117
Orders: (800) 858-2580
Tel: (402) 731-3901
Seeds for ornamental grasses, perennial and annual flowers, gourds, herbs, and vegetables for all U.S. regions.

ELIXIR FARM BOTANICALS
General Delivery
Brixey, MO 65618
Tel: (417) 261-2393
Certified biodynamic and organic Chinese and indigenous medicinals.

THE ENGLISH GARDEN EMPORIUM
Box 222
Manchester, VT 05254
Tel: (800) 347-8130
Over 200 varieties of flower and vegetable seeds imported from Johnson's Seeds of England. Importers of Seeds of Distinction —rare and unusual varieties of perennials and select annuals.

FEDCO SEEDS
P.O. Box 520
Waterville, ME 04903
Tel: (207) 873-7333
Good selection of older varieties of flowers suitable for cold climates with short seasons. $2 catalog.

THE FLOWER AND HERB EXCHANGE
3076 North Winn Road
Decorah, IA 52101
Tel: (319) 382-5990
*Dedicated to the preservation of
flowers, ornamentals, and herbs
that are family heirlooms, unusual or not available commercially.
Listed members steward such
plants and share them with other
gardeners via the Exchange. FHE
compiles one list each year that is
mailed to members, who order
directly from the member offering
the seed. There is an annual $10
membership fee ($12 Canadian,
$15 overseas).*

FLOWERY BRANCH SEED CO.
P.O. Box 1330
Flowery Branch, GA 30542
Tel: (770) 536-8380
*Strange and unusual perennials
and annuals from around the
world. Lots of herbs, including
medicinals.*

**FOX HOLLOW HERBS AND
HEIRLOOM SEED CO.**
Box 148
McGrann, PA 16236
Tel: (724) 548-SEED
*Quality organic heirloom varieties
of herbs and flowers.*

FRAGRANT PATH
P.O. Box 328
Fort Calhoun, NE 68023
*Small but interesting selection of
fragrant flowers, including herbs
and vines.*

**GRANDMA'S GARDEN,
UNDERWOOD GARDENS**
4N381 Maple Avenue
Bensenville, IL 60106
Fax: (888) 382-7041
www.grandmasgarden.com
*Good selection of rare heirloom
flowers, vegetables, and herbs, plus
tips on seed-saving and organic
growing. $3 catalog.*

HEIRLOOM SEED PROJECT
Landis Valley Museum
2451 Kissel Hill Road
Lancaster, PA 17601
Tel: (717) 569-0401
*Nonprofit organization working to
preserve plant material grown by
Pennsylvania Germans before
1940.*

HEIRLOOM SEEDS
P.O. Box 245
West Elizabeth, PA 15088
Tel: (412) 384-0852
www.heirloomseeds.com
*Seeds only of vegetables and flow-
ers, mostly of U.S. origin.*

HERITAGE ROSARIUM
211 Haviland Mill Road
Brookeville, MD 20833
Tel: (301) 774-2806
heritagero@aol.com
Large selection of old garden roses.

J.L. HUDSON, SEEDSMAN
Star Route 2, Box 337
La Honda, CA 94020
Large selection of native seeds from around the world. Species for most habitats: prairie, woodland, wetland, alpine, cool and warm deserts, dry and moist tropical, chaparral, coastal, and for a wide range of ecological niches. Also offers some rare and endangered plants.

ION EXCHANGE
1878 Old Mission Drive
Harpers Ferry, IA 52146
Order: (800) 291-2143
Tel: (319) 535-7231
Over 200 species of native plant species and over 100 species as plug and potted plants.

THOMAS JEFFERSON CENTER FOR HISTORIC PLANTS
Monticello, P.O. Box 316
Charlottesville, VA 22902
Tel: (804) 984-9821
www.monticello.org/shop
The Center collects, preserves, and sells historic plant varieties, many of which were grown by Thomas Jefferson in his gardens at Monticello. Also seed of some varieties of native American plants.

JOHNNY'S SELECTED SEEDS
310 Foss Hill Road
Albion, ME 04910
Tel: (207) 437-9294
Exceptional vegetable and heirloom flower varieties trialed in cold climates. Also medicinal herbs.

ADRIAN KENCIK
370 Frankhauser Road
Williamsville, NY 14221
Tel: (716) 633-9248
johnken1@aol.com
Enthusiastic collector and grower of rare morning glories.

LOGEE'S GREENHOUSES
141 North Street
Danielson, CT 06239
Tel: (860) 774-8038
Over 2,000 houseplants, including heirloom tropicals and subtropicals.

McCLURE AND ZIMMERMAN
100 W. Winnebago, P.O. Box 368
Friesland, WI 53935
Order: (800) 883-6998
Tel: (414) 326-4600
Quality flowerbulb brokers: bulbs suitable for restoration projects, and wild tulips and daffodils.

MOUNTAIN VALLEY GROWERS
38325 Pepperweed Road
Squaw Valley, CA 93675
Tel: (209) 338-2775
350 varieties of quality herbs and flowers, some dating back to the 1600s.

NATIONAL GARDENING ASSOCIATION
180 Flynn Avenue
Burlington, VT 05401
Tel: (802) 863-1308
www.garden.org
Offers an active seed exchange through its web site.

NATIVE SEEDS/SEARCH
526 North Fourth Avenue
Tucson, AZ 85705
Tel: (520) 327-9123
www.azstarnet.com/nss/home.
html
Members receive 10% discount on all purchases and workshops, and quarterly newsletter, The Seedhead News. *Dedicated to the preservation of endangered native plants, and to redistributing native crops, NSS hold various events at their trial gardens throughout the year. Membership $20, Family $35; low income $12, free to Native Americans.*

NEW ENGLAND WILD FLOWER SOCIETY
Garden-in-the-Woods
180 Hemenway Road
Framingham, MA 01701
Tel: (508) 877-7630
www.newfs.org
200 native plants, retail only, April 15 to September 30. Mail-order seeds, January to March 15.

NICHOLS GARDEN NURSERY
1190 North Pacific Highway
Albany, OR 97321
Tel: (541) 928-9280
Seeds of vegetables, culinary herbs, and some cottage garden flowers.

OLD HOUSE GARDENS
HEIRLOOM BULBS
536 Third Street
Ann Arbor, MI 48103
Tel: (734) 995-1486
www.oldhousegardens.com
Old varieties of tulips, daffodils, hyacinths, crocus, gladioli, cannas, and other bulbs, plus lots of historical information.
Catalog, $2.

PERENNIAL PLEASURES NURSERY
P.O. Box 147
2 Brickhouse Road
East Hardwick, VT 05836
Tel: (802) 472-5104
Field-grown perennials and herbs from the 17th, 18th, and 19th centuries.

PINETREE GARDEN SEEDS
Box 300
New Gloucester, ME 04260
Tel: (207) 926-3400
www.superseeds.com
800 varieties of seeds, including open-pollinated flowers and herbs.

PRAIRIE MOON NURSERY
Route 3, Box 163
Winona, MN 55987
Tel: (507) 452-1362
More than 400 species of seeds and plants native to North America.

REDWOOD CITY SEED COMPANY
Box 361
Redwood City, CA 94064
Tel: (650) 325-7333
www.ecoseeds.com
Seeds of open-pollinated vegetables and medicinal herbs, sweetgrass plants native to North America.

ROSES OF YESTERDAY & TODAY
802 Brown's Valley Road
Watsonville, CA 95076
Tel: (831) 724-3537
200 roses, some modern, some antique. Many hardy varieties and highly perfumed rare roses.

ROYALL RIVER ROSES
P.O. Box 370
Yarmouth, ME 04096
Tel: (800) 820-5830
Fax: (207) 846-7306
www.royallriverroses.com
230 varieties of hardy uncommon roses that flourish when grown organically.

SANTA BARBARA HEIRLOOM
SEEDLING NURSERY
P.O. Box 4235
Santa Barbara, CA 93140
Tel: (805) 968-5444
Organic growers of heirloom herbs and flowers, with some seed stock from the 1800s.

SAVORY'S GARDENS
5300 Whiting Avenue
Edina, MN 55439
Tel: (812) 941-8755
Over 1000 varieties of organic field-grown hostas, including some traditional favorites dating to the 1800s.

SEEDS OF CHANGE
P.O. Box 15700
Santa Fe, NM 87506
Tel: (888) 762-7333
Over 400 varieties of open-pollinated seeds for vegetables, flowers, and herbs, including many heirloom varieties, produced organically.

SEEDS TRUST
HIGH ALTITUDE GARDENS
P.O. Box 1048
Hailey, ID 83333
Tel: (208) 788-4419
www.seedsave.org
100 varieties adapted to cold climates.

SEEDS WEST GARDEN SEEDS
317 14th Street N.W.
Albuquerque, NM 87104
Tel: (505) 843-9713
www.seedswestgardenseeds.com
Mail order seeds, specializing in heirloom, open-pollinated, and gourmet organically grown vegetable seeds for short-growing-season gardening. Also an excellent traditional flower collection.

SELECT SEEDS
ANTIQUE FLOWERS
180 Stickney Hill Road
Union, CT 06076
Tel: (860) 684-9310
Flowers from the 18th and 19th centuries; over 100 varieties of annuals and perennials.

SHEPHERD'S GARDEN SEEDS
30 Irene Street
Torrington, CT 06790
Tel: (860) 482-3638
www.shepherdseeds.com
Specialty seeds plus unique varieties of flowers and herbs from around the world chosen for flavor, easy culture, quality, and high germination. Exclusive heritage sweet peas.

SOUTHERN EXPOSURE
SEED EXCHANGE
P.O. Box 170
Earlysville, VA 22936
Tel: (804) 973-4703
www.southernexposure.com
*Encouraging seed exchange by
information and supplies; open-
pollinated seed of rare, endangered and heirloom herb and
flower varieties. Seed list $1.00.*

THOMPSON & MORGAN
Box 1308
Jackson, NJ 08527
Tel: (908) 363-2225
*Over 2,000 varieties, including
many rare and unusual plants.*

ANDRE VIETTE FARM & NURSERY
P.O. Box 1109
Fishersville, VA 22939
Tel: (540) 943-2315
*Rare and exotic perennials from
the United States and Europe.*

VINTAGE GARDENS
2833 Old Gravenstein Hwy. S.
Sebastopol, CA 95472
Tel: (707) 829-2035
*Nearly 2,000 roses, all rated for
fragrance and blooming habits.*

WE-DU NURSERIES
Rt. 5, Box 724
Marion, NC 28752
Tel: (828) 738-8300
*Plants only; woody natives and
perennials, ferns, trillium, iris,
and many wildflowers.*

WELL SWEEP HERB FARM
205 Mt. Bethel Road
Port Murray, NJ 07865
Tel: (908) 852-5390
*Excellent source for lavender:
more than 50 species, some quite
rare.*

CONTRIBUTORS

BEVERLY DOBSON grew roses in Westchester County, New York, for 26 years before moving to California in 1994. She began publishing rose information in the 1970s and founded the *Combined Rose List* in 1980. She is an American Rose Society Accredited Judge and Consulting Rosarian, and the only American Honorary Vice President of the Royal National Rose Society.

For the last 18 years, **RACHEL KANE** has run Perennial Pleasures Nursery in East Hardwick, Vermont, which specializes in rare heirloom perennials. In her determination to collect vintage plants, she has imported many 18th- and 19th-century cultivars from Britain. Rachel has worked on a consulting basis for many garden restorations.

SCOTT KUNST is the owner of Old House Gardens, the country's only mail-order source devoted to heirloom bulbs. A landscape historian and preservationist, he has taught landscape history at Eastern Michigan University and has been helping historic-house museums and home-owners restore their grounds for over 15 years. Scott, his wife, and their two sons live in a 1889 Queen Anne house in Ann Arbor, Michigan.

TOVAH MARTIN'S interest in heirlooms began with indoor plants at Logee's Greenhouses in Danielson, Connecticut, where she spent more than 20 years caring for the vintage begonia collection. She is the garden editor of *Victoria* magazine and the *Litchfield County Times*. Her writing has appeared frequently in the Sunday *New York Times*, and she is the author of several gardening books, including *Tasha Tudor's Garden* (Houghton Mifflin Co., 1994). She is the guest editor of two previous BBG handbooks, *Greenhouses and Garden Rooms* (1989) and *A New Look at Houseplants* (1995).

CHRISTIE WHITE researches, plans, and plants re-created kitchen and ornamental gardens for the historic houses in Old Sturbridge Village in Sturbridge, Massachusetts. She also supervises the Village's herb garden collection of over 400 varieties. Christie lectures extensively on early- 19th-century gardens and heirloom plants.

PHOTO CREDITS

DAVID CAVAGNARO
cover and pages 1, 13, 20, 25, 26, 28, 33, 34, 36, 38, 39 (top and bottom), 43, 45, 47, 48, 50 (top and bottom), 51, 52 (top and bottom), 59, 63, 66, 68, 71, 73, 76, 80, 84 (top left and bottom), 94

ALAN & LINDA DETRICK
pages 17, 22, 27, 31, 37, 41, 49, 64 (left), 67 (right), 69, 70, 84 (top right)

SCOTT KUNST
pages 7, 8, 9, 11, 14 (left and right), 15

TOVAH MARTIN
pages 5, 55, 57, 79, 83, 87, 91, 93

JERRY PAVIA
pages 24, 29, 44, 53, 61, 62, 64 (right), 67 (left), 75, 88

BILL STITES
pages 92, 95

Escape the kill zone. Easier said than done!

Connor tapped his mic. "Alpha One to Control. Request emergency EVAC."

His earpiece burst into life, and he heard Charley, Alpha team's operations leader, respond, *"Alpha One, this is Control. Backup on its way. Three minutes out."*

Three minutes? thought Connor. They'd be dead meat in that time. And, without any firepower of their own, they were defenseless. Connor needed an exit strategy . . . and fast.

Covering the Principal with his body, Connor peeked over the wall and scanned the immediate area. A clump of bushes off to their right gave some visual cover for an escape, but no physical protection from gunfire. A car parked farther down the street provided little hope; he was too young to know how to drive, let alone know how to hot-wire a car! He looked at the building behind them—a small warehouse with offices attached. The back entrance was only thirty feet away, but it was across open ground. Checking on the enemy's progress, Connor saw that the shooter behind the tree was advancing to get a clear shot. He had no choice but to risk it.

"Move!" he growled, seizing his Principal by the arm and sprinting toward the warehouse.

Keeping his body close, Connor shielded the boy as the enemy opened fire. Bullets whizzed past. One almost clipped his ear. Their feet pounded across the pavement and, whether through speed or pure luck, they made it to the entrance unharmed.

Connor yanked on the handle. "NO!" he cried, tugging furiously at the locked doors.

He spun around. They were now sitting ducks. Connor shoved his Principal into the shelter of a large wheeled Dumpster. The boy tried to run on, crying, "I don't want to die!"

"Stay down," Connor ordered, pushing him to the ground. Then through clenched teeth he added, "Amir, you're not making this any easier for me."

"Sorry," replied his friend, offering a flash of a grin from behind his safety goggles. "But I'm supposed to be a panicking Principal."

"Well, panic *less*," Connor pleaded as several bullets thudded into the metal bin.

Amir flinched and covered his head with his arms. "A bit difficult under the circumstances, don't you think?"

Richie, who was playing the part of the first shooter in the training scenario, had left his position in the alley and was unleashing a hail of paintballs from his assault rifle. So was Ling, the other shooter, who by now had reached the far end of the low wall. If either of them managed to hit Amir with even a single paintball, Connor would instantly fail the exercise.

Ever since his successful assignment protecting the American president's daughter the month before, the rest of Alpha team had been impressed but also a little envious of his newly acquired status. The only other person on the team to have earned a gold Guardian badge was Charley—and she truly deserved it, whereas he was just a first-time rookie.

That's why certain fellow guardians had made it their mission to test him to the limit—in Ling's words, "to make sure Connor doesn't get too big for his boots." Although Connor had no problem with a bit of good-natured teasing, deep down he questioned whether his first assignment had just been beginner's luck. It was true his father had been in the Special Air Service, a unit of the British Special Forces, and been one of the best bodyguards on the circuit. But that didn't mean Connor was made of the same stuff. For his own peace of mind, he needed to prove himself . . . beyond a doubt.

Connor clicked his mic again. "Alpha One to Control. Where's my pickup?"

"Alpha One. Thirty seconds out. Maintain position."

As more paintballs thudded into the bin and splattered the pavement at their feet, Connor wondered, *Do I have any other choice?*

Richie closed in, setting his sights on Amir. Connor pressed

Amir farther down behind the dumpster. Paintballs rattled off it like hailstones. A black 4×4 Range Rover roared down the road, its tires screeching as the driver braked hard and spun the armored vehicle to form a shield against Richie's attack. The paintballs now pinged harmlessly off the bodywork.

But that still left Ling as a threat. With fifteen meters of open ground between them, she *couldn't* miss her target. Connor realized he was in a no-win situation. Whether they ran or stayed put, one or both of them would be shot down.

Then Connor had an idea. Kicking off the Dumpster's brakes, he grabbed Amir and shoved the huge container with his shoulder.

"What on earth are you doing?" cried Amir as the wheeled Dumpster began rolling down the path toward the Range Rover and Connor pushed him ahead to stay covered.

"Getting rid of the garbage," replied Connor with a grin as the Dumpster resounded with the furious impact of Ling's paintballs. The Dumpster was picking up speed now, and Connor and Amir had to sprint alongside it to stay shielded from Ling's assault. Then the Dumpster struck the wall and came to a dead stop. Having lost their only cover, the two of them made a final mad dash for the Range Rover.

Paintballs peppered the hood and windshield as Connor wrenched the back door open and shoved Amir inside.

Connor dived in after him, landing on top of him in the footwell.

"GO! GO! GO!" he screamed at the driver.

Flooring the accelerator, the driver sped away from the kill zone.

ACKNOWLEDGMENTS

This second installment in the Bodyguard series was made possible by the hard work and commitment of:

Brian Geffen, my editor at Philomel Books, who has helped to produce an even punchier edition of this story. I just wish I'd written the extra chapters the first time around!

Michael Green, Publisher, whose support and vision has made a US edition of the Bodyguard series possible.

Laurel Robinson, my copyeditor, whose honing skills have given the final manuscript a razor-sharp edge!

And of course you, my readers who have hopefully read the first installment, *Recruit*, and been immediately compelled to pick up this one and tell all your friends about it!

Read, enjoy and stay safe!
— Chris

Any fans can keep in touch with me via my YouTube channel ChrisBradfordAuthor or the website www.chrisbradford.co.uk

BROOKLYN BOTANIC GARDEN

MORE

BOOKS ON

FABULOUS

FLOWERS

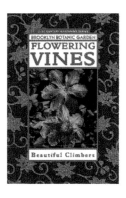

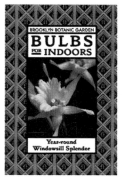